Story Skeleton

The Classics

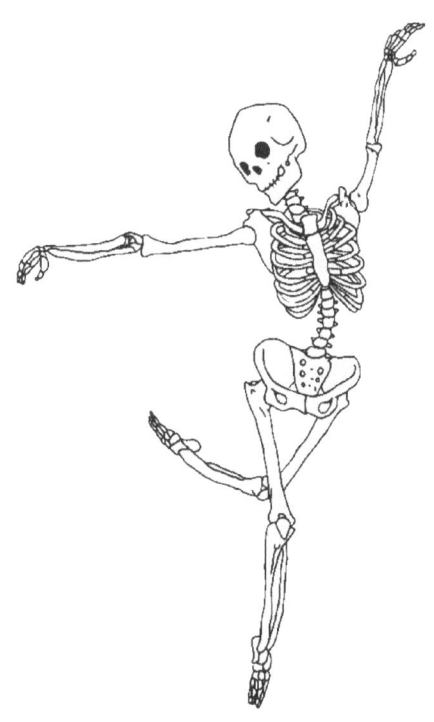

by David Griffin Brown and Michelle Barker

Praise for *Immersion and Emotion: The Two Pillars of Storytelling*

☆☆☆☆☆
"I highly recommend it for writers of all skill levels."

☆☆☆☆☆
"Michelle Barker and David Griffin Brown have crafted a literary gem that deserves a permanent spot on every writer's bookshelf."

☆☆☆☆☆
"This book is a treasure trove for both aspiring writers and seasoned authors, offering profound insights into the art of creating immersive and emotionally resonant narratives."

☆☆☆☆☆
"If you aspire to craft stories that captivate and resonate, this book is an indispensable companion."

☆☆☆☆☆
"Clear, concise, and jam-packed with practical insight."

Bonus chapter included at the end of this book!

Darling Axe Publishing

DarlingAxe.com

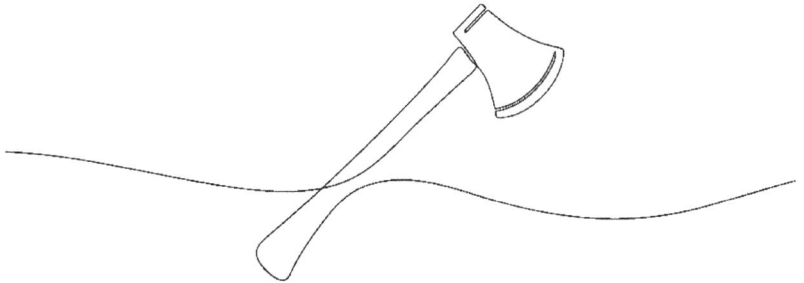

Copyright © 2025 David Griffin Brown

Copyright © 2025 Michelle Barker

ISBN: 978-1-7380766-5-9

Cover designed by MiblArt.com.

All rights reserved.

Contents

Introduction 7

I. Keeping It (Relatively) Simple 5

    Moby-Dick and Alice's Adventures in Wonderland 6

    The Old Man and the Sea 16

    Giovanni's Room 25

    The Picture of Dorian Gray 37

    Pride and Prejudice 50

    Of Mice and Men 63

II. Getting Creative 77

    The Great Gatsby 78

    The Scarlet Letter 86

    The Call of the Wild 104

    Madame Bovary 117

    Heart of Darkness 131

III. Cracking the Code 147

    Jane Eyre 148

    The Bell Jar 156

    As I Lay Dying 169

    To the Lighthouse 183

    Animal Farm 195

    The Godfather 204

    Middlemarch 220

    Wuthering Heights 238

    Brideshead Revisited 252

Introduction

First Things First—A Little About Us

Hello, fellow storytellers! We are David Brown and Michelle Barker, senior editors at the Darling Axe. We met in the MFA program at the University of British Columbia, then joined forces in 2018. Since then, we have spent countless hours thinking about story structure: what works, what doesn't, and why. At first, we only did this with our own work and with our clients' manuscripts. But soon it occurred to us: maybe it would be instructive to take a look at how master storytellers have done it. Maybe they have something to teach us.

All right, there was also a bit of a challenge in it. On occasion, various books had come up in discussions with clients who said, "But there's no structure in this one. There's no plot." And we thought, *but there must be a plot. And we're going to find it.*

And so we did.

The Art of the Novel

The structure of a novel is central to its artistry.

In order to understand how a novel has been written, we must understand its anatomy. If we think of a novel as a body, the structure is its skeleton. It's what supports and connects all the disparate pieces into one marvelous whole.

Aristotle kept the idea of novel structure simple: a story has a beginning, a middle, and an end. While three-act structure is the backbone of most storytelling, there can be endless variation in how this structure is handled. Here's another metaphor: think of story structure as a painter's canvas—the four edges may represent a limitation, but infinite creativity can take place within those bounds.

As Orson Welles once said, "The absence of limitations is the enemy of art."

Story structure also relates to the psychological appeal of narrative, that which engages readers and builds in them a sense of anticipation—a desire to know what happens next. A strong narrative structure creates emotional draw in the reader. It makes them invested in the story, keeps them turning pages. In short, it makes them care—and that, it turns out, is our number one job as authors. We must make our readers care.

For that reason, Story Skeletons are a valuable subject of study. The classics, in particular, have stood the test of time. They are classics for a reason, not least of which is the way their authors handled story structure. They found ways to make us care, and they did it so effectively that we have continued to care—for decades, even centuries after the novels were written. It's an impressive feat.

How to Read This Book

William Faulkner said, "Read, read, read. Read everything—trash, classics, good and bad, and see how they do it. Just like a carpenter who works as an apprentice and studies the master." That is what we're doing here.

Each of the twenty-one novels and novellas we've chosen has something to teach us. We will be touching on a variety of structures and features, from straightforward narratives to novels with multiple storylines, from those that function as allegories to those that feature unreliable narrators. Some are organized by setting; others are episodic. Some use a frame narrative; others employ several trajectories or mess with the placement of the inciting incident. There are many ways to write a great novel.

For that reason, it's worthwhile to read all the Skeletons, not just the ones from the novels you're familiar with. Each has something significant to offer that will elevate your writing. We've written each chapter in such a way that you don't need to have read the book to understand the structure. That being said, we still recommend you read all these books. It's one thing to break them down on a theoretical level, but another entirely to see how the structure comes together on the page.

And to quote Stephen King: "If you don't have time to read, you don't have the time (or the tools) to write."

The Connection Between Structure and Emotional Draw

What do things like the midpoint or the inciting incident have to do with a reader's emotional investment in the story? It sounds like a nerdy riddle. The connection is certainly counterintuitive. But in fact, structure and emotional draw are directly connected.

A protagonist's narrative goal creates empathy. When we know what the protagonist wants, we are more likely to relate to them; we root for them to achieve their goal. We become even more invested if the stakes are high—and if they're personal. Internal conflict strengthens our connection to the protagonist and creates additional external conflict.

The obstacles that occur in the story's rising action create tension, suspense, and uncertainty. We don't know what will happen, but we want to know. Add to that a sense of causality, which creates momentum. The protagonist's actions and reactions determine what will happen next. Their predicament keeps getting worse—at least partly because they keep making it worse.

Everything builds to the climax. The whole story leads to this moment: will the protagonist achieve their goal? Or will they lose everything? Will they experience transformation in the nick of time, or will it happen too late for them to get what they wanted? And perhaps they don't get what they want in the end—but they get what they need.

Cracking the Code

A novel's structural elements can be organized strategically, creatively, unusually—but in a satisfying narrative, they're all there in some form. That form might be surprising when you realize what the author has really done—which often isn't clear the first or even second time you read a complex novel. But once you crack the code, it's immensely satisfying.

As a side note, while writing this book we often sent each other excited texts that simply read: *OMG I cracked the code!!!!* Whenever it happened, it was an excellent moment.

With that, let's get started cracking the codes of these wonderful classic novels and novellas.

Part One: Keeping It (Relatively) Simple

We figured starting with novels that employ a fairly simple three-act structure would be a good way to get our feet wet. This will familiarize you with all the elements of three-act structure and how they shake out in practical terms.

But we do say *relatively* simple. In each of these novels, if the structure is straightforward, you can count on there being something else going on that lifts the novel out of the ordinary and into the extraordinary.

Each of these authors has done something remarkable with their work. In the novels and novellas in this section, we'll be looking at things like internal conflict, as well as the art of writing a novel that supports multiple interpretations. We'll examine a novel that breaks new ground in both the romance genre and with POV, and we'll consider the potential for imagery in repeating motifs.

Moby-Dick and Alice's Adventures in Wonderland

by Herman Melville and Lewis Carroll

White Whale, White Rabbit

Alice's Adventures in Wonderland and *Moby-Dick* have a surprising amount in common, at least in terms of narrative structure. Of course, both also have protagonists chasing after a symbolic white animal. In Ahab's case, the whale represents vengeance. For Alice, the rabbit represents the unbridled curiosity of youth.

The structure of both of these novels is exceedingly simple. In fact, the mastery in each is evident in this simplicity. Few authors can pull off a straight-shot trajectory. By this we mean neither novel has a true subplot. Alice moves through a number of episodic encounters, and Ahab's pursuit of Moby Dick is given complexity through Ishmael, the famously unreliable narrator—and his friend Queequeg to an extent. But in the end, each protagonist chases their quarry from start to finish without significant relationship arcs or secondary narrative goals. That's why we thought it made sense to start off with a side-by-side comparison of these two books.

For most authors, a straight-shot trajectory can result in a shrunken story world that does not reflect the complexity and wonderful messiness of life. But anything can be done well, especially when it's intentional. The structural complexity that might otherwise seem lacking in *Alice's Adventures in Wonderland* is made up for with rich descriptions, wildly surrealistic landscapes, and childlike poetry. And poetry—plus deeply symbolic parable—is the heart of Herman Melville's masterpiece.

Narrative Goal

Let's take a closer look at the mechanics of these two novels, starting with a couple loglines:

- When young Alice follows a rabbit in a waistcoat down into Wonderland, she must brave the dangers and riddles of mystifying creatures and locales—culminating in an encounter with the decapitation-obsessed Queen of Hearts—or else she may never find her way home.

- After an initial violent encounter with a massive white whale in which he loses a leg, Captain Ahab sets off to hunt Moby Dick and exact his revenge, even if it costs him his life and his crew.

The protagonist in both novels has a clear narrative goal, something they struggle toward over the course of the novel. For Alice, it is the White Rabbit; for Ahab, it's Moby Dick.

PLOT POINTS

Stasis

A story's stasis provides context and shows us the protagonist's normal life before it all gets knocked sideways. The stasis can also reveal a core impulse that will develop into a narrative goal. However, not all novels begin in stasis. Some start before, some after.

Alice's stasis is brief. She sits by a riverbank, feeling bored and drowsy. She half-heartedly watches her sister read a book without pictures—a mundanity that doesn't interest Alice at all. She drifts in and out of her thoughts, wondering about trivial things like whether it would be worth making a daisy chain to pass the time. Here is her underlying motivation: she is bored and thus wishes for excitement.

In *Moby-Dick*, the story opens later, just before the threshold or the point of no return. As such, Ahab's stasis is implied—it's the time before he lost his leg to Moby Dick, and long before he sets out on his quest for vengeance.

Inciting Incident

The inciting incident of a novel is the moment when the protagonist's underlying motivation crystallizes into their narrative goal. It is sometimes referred to as the catalyst because it's the event that occurs to disrupt the stasis. However, as we will see in other novels, the catalyst and the inciting incident can be two separate plot points. Note that the inciting incident is the first link in a causal chain that will culminate in the climax.

Alice's story begins when she sees the White Rabbit. He's wearing a waistcoat, checking his pocket watch, and muttering about how he's late. Her curiosity overtakes her, and thus her narrative goal is formed: she will follow this rabbit to find out more about him. Her choice sets the story in motion, as it leads her to the rabbit hole—a portal into Wonderland. This moment is the turning point that pulls her from the stasis of her monotonous everyday life into the whimsical, chaotic adventure ahead.

Ahab's story begins when he first encounters the notorious whale. Note, again, that Ahab's inciting incident happens prior to the beginning of the novel. Moby Dick has already won the first round, smashing Ahab's boat, killing many of his crew, and leaving the captain maimed. His narrative goal is simple: he will find this whale, and he will have his revenge.

Point of No Return

After the inciting incident, a protagonist should find themselves in a situation where it's no longer possible to return to life as it once was. Maybe technically they could go back, but emotionally they can't.

Alice's point of no return immediately follows her inciting incident. After crawling into a dark hole to find out what the White Rabbit is late for, she falls into Wonderland. Going back isn't possible. She must see this journey through.

In *Moby-Dick*, the story begins just before the point of no return. Ahab is getting his boat and crew ready for the big hunt. He crosses the threshold when they set sail. This is an example of an emotional point of no return. Ahab could decide to chill out and give up on this mad quest, but his desire for revenge is too great.

Rising Action

Rising action involves the obstacles a protagonist meets while on the path toward their goal. It consists of a chain of consequences, a series of actions and reactions. As the protagonist struggles and strives toward the goal, they are tested, and through these tests they reveal who they are to the reader. This is a crucial source of character connection.

In every chapter, Alice meets a new obstacle—a puzzle she needs to unravel or characters she must engage with on her way to finding the White Rabbit.

Ahab's rising action isn't as easy to define, especially since he's not the narrator. For most of the book, he's holed up below deck, leaving the hard work to his men so he can stew on his vengeful anger. As for the crew, they are hunting a whale: the obstacles are time and distance. Consequently, Melville structures the story around a series of meetings between the *Pequod* and nine other ships, each of which offers fodder for symbolic interpretation.

All Is Lost? Or a False Victory?

Plot points correspond to emotional turns in the reader. The inciting incident generates the goal, giving us a reason to cheer the protagonist onward. The point of no return represents a deeper commitment to the goal, and thus an acceptance of the stakes. Now the reader has a reason to fear the protagonist's potential failure. Rising action pits the protagonist against external AND internal conflict, which ratchets up the stakes and thus the tension.

The next plot point can go in one of two ways: to an all-is-lost moment or a false victory. Which one it will be depends on whether the story is a tragedy or a comedy—comedy in the old-school Greek dramaturgy sense, not in the humorous sense. In a comic structure, the protagonist will achieve their narrative goal, though they will have to transform in some way first. The plot point we see here is an all-is-lost moment. In a tragedy, the protagonist will meet with failure in the climax, and their transformation will follow—they transform as a result of their failure. Therefore, a tragic climax is preceded by a false victory.

In an all-is-lost moment, the protagonist hits rock bottom—they are brought closest to failure. In a false victory, it seems like everything will be okay... right before it all goes to hell. Either way, the emotional volume increases, such that the climax hits as hard as possible.

Throughout Alice's journey in Wonderland, her narrative goal has been shifting. She's still searching for the rabbit, but she's doing so with decreasing enthusiasm. Wonderland is absurd, frustrating, and even dangerous. This is especially true when she reaches the court of the Queen of Hearts. She has found the White Rabbit at last, but he is absorbed in his duties as a herald and pays her no mind. And now she must contend with the Queen and all her chaos.

Alice's all-is-lost moment comes during the trial. The Knave of Hearts has been accused of stealing the Queen's tarts. The trial is ridiculous: evidence is nonsensical, the witnesses are unreliable, and the rules are arbitrary. Alice initially tries to play along, but her frustration builds as she recognizes the trial's absurdity and the injustice of the Queen's behavior.

She can no longer tolerate the madness around her, and this leads to her final transformation. She is done following whimsy through Wonderland, and now she wants to go home.

Moby-Dick, on the other hand, is a tragedy, so Ahab gets a false victory rather than an all-is-lost moment. The crew has searched long and far for the White Whale, and there's never been any guarantee of finding the beast. It's a big ocean, after all. The potential failure for Ahab is that they never encounter Moby Dick and his vengeance goes unfulfilled. The false victory occurs when the crew of the *Pequod* finally sights the White Whale after months of relentless pursuit. As Ahab beholds the object of his hatred, it seems like the realization of his vengeance quest is at hand.

Climax

The climax answers a question that was asked in the inciting incident: will the protagonist succeed, or will they fail while learning something important?

Alice has realized that what she wanted is not what she needs. It was whimsy, innocence, and curiosity that prompted her to follow the White Rabbit, but Wonderland has taught her some important lessons. The mundane world, with its pictureless books and quiet riverbanks, has an appeal after all in its normalcy and predictability. When she rejects Wonderland internally, her transformation is expressed externally—she grows taller and taller and shouts, "You're nothing but a pack of cards." Indeed, in rejecting Wonderland, she has grown up, if just a bit.

Since *Moby-Dick* is a tragedy, Ahab doesn't transform before the climax. He forges on with his fatal flaw. He and his crew attack the White Whale, and they lose. The ship is smashed to pieces, and apart from the narrator Ishmael, every last crew member is lost. Ahab's transformation is a mortal one. Presumably he learns a lesson in defeat, even as he sinks below the waves.

Resolution

In a novel's resolution, we take a step beyond the causality that connects the inciting incident to the climax. This is where loose ends are tied off and the author leaves us with a final image of the transformed protagonist as well as a closing sentiment. This might also be where the author drops a hint about a sequel.

After Alice shouts at the Queen's court, the cards swarm her. But the chaotic scene quickly ends, and she wakes up on the riverbank and tells her sister about her wild dream. Alice then runs off, and we get a quiet moment of contemplation with her sister in which she imagines Alice as an adult, recounting her whimsical adventure to children. The implication is that Alice's wonder and imagination may persist even as she grows up.

After Ahab's death and the destruction of the ship, Ishmael is left floating alone in the vast ocean. He clings to his friend Queequeg's coffin, a symbol of death that becomes his salvation. Days later, he is rescued by the *Rachel,* a whaling ship still searching for its own lost crew members. The resolution is both somber and contemplative. Ishmael is left to tell the tale of Ahab's destructive obsession and the catastrophic end of the *Pequod*.

The Arc of Triumph—and Failure

Experiences change us. A character at the end of a story is not the same as they were at the beginning.

Alice begins her adventure with childlike curiosity—without fear. Over the course of her adventures, she learns that curiosity can lead to exciting discoveries and encounters, but it can also lead to danger. In a sense, this is a seven-year-old's revelation that the world isn't as safe as she might have imagined, even if there is much that awaits her discovery.

Ahab doesn't have a true arc, but the story isn't about him, even if he owns the trajectory. Instead, Ishmael bears witness to the destructive consequences of revenge. In other words, Ishmael learns a valuable lesson on Ahab's behalf. Even more, the reader experiences this arc, since Ishmael's often slippery narration casts doubt on whether any of his story should be believed in the first place. The story's conclusion hangs in the air with more questions than answers. Is this, in fact, a story about the perils of revenge, or is it about the ephemeral nature of narrative itself?

Why Are *Moby-Dick* and *Alice's Adventures in Wonderland* Classics?

Alice's Adventures in Wonderland is random, silly, and fun. What it lacks in narrative complexity it makes up for with rich descriptions and boundless creativity. Even among children's literature, this is an unusual approach to storytelling—although the sheer randomness of the plot is often cited as a reason some people don't connect with the book.

Alice's quest is exceedingly simple: *follow the White Rabbit*. There's actually not much causality from one scene to the next. In that sense, the story can be described as anecdotal, which runs afoul of much craft advice. Still, the classic persists, and no doubt the fascination with Alice's encounters can be credited to Lewis Carroll's vibrant imagination.

Moby-Dick is an incredibly complex novel with symbols and themes that scholars still argue over. What's amazing about this book is that the narrative trajectory is sidelined by its experimental form.

Though there is no story without Ahab, it is the narrator Ishmael's wide-ranging literary devices, soliloquies, footnotes, and breathtaking poetry that beget the novel's true appeal. It is less the story itself and more the telling of the tale that makes it worth reading. That is a mark of true mastery in the art of novel writing.

Chapter Summary: As the Crow Flies

Melville's *Moby-Dick* and Carroll's *Alice's Adventures in Wonderland*, though vastly different in tone and genre, share a surprising commonality in their narrative structures. Both feature protagonists who pursue a singular, symbolic white creature, driving a straightforward trajectory without significant subplots.

Plot as a Series of Emotional Pivots: Plot points are more than just events in a story; they correspond to shifts in the reader's emotions. Each plot point—from the inciting incident to the climax—is crafted to elicit specific emotional responses, connecting readers to the protagonist and making us care about their journey.

An Emotional Hook: The inciting incident disrupts the protagonist's stasis and crystallizes their underlying motivation into a clear narrative goal. This moment hooks readers by generating excitement and curiosity, compelling us to invest emotionally in the story.

Point of No Return: The point of no return (also known as the doorway of no return or the threshold) is a pivotal plot point in which the protagonist makes a decisive choice that irreversibly commits them to the central conflict, making it impossible to return to their former life, whether physically or emotionally. This amplifies the stakes and heightens the readers' emotional investment, as we now share in the protagonist's commitment to the journey ahead.

Rising Tension and Connection: The rising action presents obstacles and challenges that test the protagonist. As they struggle and strive, they reveal their character, and so readers form a stronger emotional connection as we cheer the protagonist onward.

All-Is-Lost Moment Versus False Victory: Approaching the climax, the story reaches a critical emotional staging ground—either an all-is-lost scenario or a false victory. This plot point intensifies emotions like despair or fleeting relief, setting the stage for the ultimate resolution and maximizing the impact of the climax.

The End of the Narrative Bridge: The climax answers the central question posed by the inciting incident: Will the protagonist achieve their goal? Or will they fail while learning an important lesson?

Falling Action: The resolution ties up loose ends and underscores the protagonist's transformation. It leaves the reader with a final emotional impression, whether it's contemplation, satisfaction, catharsis, or even melancholy.

The Old Man and the Sea

by Ernest Hemingway

An Old Man, the Sea—What Could Be Simpler?

The hallmark of Hemingway's writing is spareness and simplicity, and yet he still manages to convey deep emotion and create connection with his characters as well as deliver a novella that is brimming with symbolism. Why? Partly because he uses the *right* words, but also because he gives the reader space to think. His writing is, like haiku, all about juxtaposition—placing things side by side and allowing the reader to make the connections. So if the structure of *The Old Man and the Sea* is simple, the meaning behind it is anything but.

If you believe the CIA, this was Saddam Hussein's favorite book because it's all about persevering despite the odds and not being defeated. In fact, this was Hemingway's last published major work of fiction. The fact that it's about having faith and not giving up becomes tragically ironic in the face of his eventual suicide.

I Once Caught a Fish This Big

The Old Man and the Sea originated as a story passed down by fishermen for decades. Who knows how big the marlin really was originally, or if there even was one. Hemingway first wrote it as a magazine piece and then decided to turn it into a novella. But he was also a fisherman himself, and that comes through in the authenticity of every tiny detail aboard the skiff.

The novella was published to rave reviews and won a Pulitzer, though critics have since soured somewhat on the book's merits. Is it an allegory about writing? About religion? Is it a story about companionship and loneliness? Or is it exactly what it looks like: a tale about a man, a boy, and a fish?

Our answer to all of the above is: yes. This novella can be read in so many ways, it is guaranteed to satisfy English teachers for centuries. But we think what it's really about is opposing forces: life and death, companionship and loneliness, youth and age. Santiago references an arm-wrestling competition at the midpoint, which reinforces the story's guiding rhythm of push and pull.

But let's start with structure.

Narrative Goal

The narrative goal is deceptively simple. An old man, Santiago, has gone eighty-four days without a catch. He has very little food or money left. This is a question of survival. Catch something or starve. The goal is clear, the stakes are high.

And he does catch something. And then he loses it.

It seems like this should be a *man versus nature* story, but Santiago's thoughts about not only the marlin but also the sea and other wildlife emphasize that nature is not his adversary. Even the sharks that eat the marlin are only doing what sharks do. Santiago is the protagonist of the story, and even while he tries to catch the marlin, he speaks of the fish as his brother. He knows his place in the circle of life. He is old, but Manolin, who adores him and helps him, is young, suggesting the boy will eventually take his place in that circle.

But the antagonist is also Santiago. He works against himself, his limitations, the challenge of sustaining pain and not surrendering to it. Throughout his time on the boat, he talks to himself, by turns encouraging and berating himself while he tries to hold on to the marlin. He even talks to his one uncooperative hand that betrays him when he needs it most.

PLOT POINTS

The novella takes place over five days and demonstrates the power not only of a strong and clear narrative goal but also of a contained and limited setting.

Stasis

After enduring eighty-four days without a fish, Santiago is determined to break his streak of bad luck, and on the eighty-fifth day he decides to sail out farther than the other skiffs to catch a big one. His stasis motivation is to catch a fish. Any fish will do.

Inciting Incident

After sailing beyond all the other boats, he snags a huge marlin on one of his lines. His narrative goal takes shape: he will best this giant fish and bring it home.

Point of No Return

Santiago decides to let the fish pull him far out to sea instead of trying to break free or turn back. This decision, made as he realizes the fish's immense strength and determination, commits him fully to the struggle.

Rising Action

The marlin doesn't make this easy for Santiago. If the old man is going to hold on to the fish, he will have to use all his strength, skill, and determination.

He catches a tuna, which he eats to keep up his strength. A warbler lands on the fishing line, and Santiago speaks to it. The marlin suddenly jumps, and he realizes it's the biggest fish he's ever seen.

Midpoint

A midpoint in a narrative is a crucial plot point occurring roughly halfway through the story. It serves to escalate the stakes, deepen the conflict, or pivot the direction of the narrative. In this case, the midpoint serves as a structural fulcrum. It is here when Santiago remembers the all-night arm-wrestling competition he won in a final burst of strength when he was younger. This doesn't seem like a significant plot point, but in terms of the rhythms of the story, it is key. Up to now, the focus has been on Santiago being pulled by the marlin. But that is about to shift.

Rising Action

The waiting game is over; now the old man must call on that final burst of strength to defeat his prey. The marlin jumps out of the water repeatedly, until Santiago is finally able to harpoon it.

False Victory

He has caught the biggest fish of his life. He lashes it to the side of the boat and begins the long journey back to land. His hands are cut up and he's exhausted, but he'll make a lot of money from this fish.

Tragic Climax

And then the sharks come. Hemingway makes an interesting shift here. Up to now, Santiago has felt a kinship with the animals. Although he was trying to catch (and kill) the marlin, he respects it and even humanizes it. But the sharks are different. They are aggressive, like blunt weapons, and the marlin becomes less noble and more like meat. Santiago apologizes to the marlin for having caught it, for having been too proud and gone out too far.

By the time he arrives back in the harbor, the sharks have devoured the marlin and nothing of it remains except the tail, backbone, spear, and head, which later gets chopped up to use in fish traps. Santiago carries his mast up the hill (very much like Christ with the cross), "destroyed but not defeated."

Resolution

Santiago returns to his shack and goes to sleep. Manolin is overjoyed to see he's alive and promises to work with him again on his boat. Even though his parents forbade him from working with the old man because he was unlucky, Manolin decides from now on *he* will bring the luck.

Hemingway suggests that the boy returns out of both loyalty and admiration for the old man—but also out of love. Manolin thought the old man had died at sea and is overwhelmed by emotion to find him safely returned.

While traditionally, Manolin's name (like Santiago's) has been given a Christian interpretation (Manolin → Manuel → Immanuel, which means "God is with us"), it can also be seen as a Spanish diminutive of the word *mano*, or hand. Santiago's hands are injured in his battle with the marlin. Manolin returns to become Santiago's hands.

At the very end, the POV shifts, and two strangers mistake the marlin skeleton for that of a shark.

The final image is of Santiago dreaming about lions.

Yes, Lions

The lions show up three times in the book—once near the beginning, once at the midpoint, and once at the end. Lions are predators, but the ones in Santiago's dreams play on the shores of a beach in Africa. They are young, and they remind him of his youth and give him both strength and hope. But this is also a novella about opposing forces, and the lions—predators that are playful—represent a union of these forces.

An Allegory of the Writer's Life?

Eighty-four days without a catch was also the essence of Hemingway's professional situation. He hadn't had a successful book in over a decade. Critics thought he was done. The story can be read as an allegory of his writing career. This is a question of survival, but it's also a question of pride—and luck. The eighty-fifth day will surely be the lucky one; i.e., *if I light that candle and recite this incantation to the muse, I will get the next big idea*.

Luck is an interesting theme in the story because everything about it is random. What does the number eighty-five signify? About the same as a row of sharpened pencils. Nothing. Santiago used to be lucky—just like Hemingway—until he wasn't. And then he caught the marlin, and his luck returned. And then he lost it, and there went his luck. It's a query-rejection-acceptance-rejection pattern that should be familiar to most writers.

Santiago sacrifices everything by going out farther than any of the other fishermen. He's going to catch the big idea. The sea, the deep unconscious, is where those ideas hide. He's spent years honing his skill. He knows how to reel it in, get it under control. He knows how to suffer for a cause.

And he catches it—and then critics attack the shit out of it until all that's left are the bones. And the author has ended up sacrificing everything (like the Christ figure at the end), and what do they have? The faith that they did their best, that they weren't defeated (though in Hemingway's case, that's debatable). And quite possibly, the opinions of strangers who totally misunderstand what they were trying to do.

Push and Pull

This movement is essential to the rhythm of the novella, not only in the catching of the fish but also thematically: loneliness versus companionship, death versus life, old age versus youth, the ebb and flow of the tide, eating and being eaten, predator and prey.

Technically, Santiago is alone at sea, and yet he also says no one is alone at sea. He's connected to the fish, the birds, and the sea itself, which he characterizes as a woman. But he is also lonely. He repeats several times that he wishes the boy were there. He doesn't have the boy to talk to anymore, so he talks to himself, to the fish, to the warbler that lands on the boat. He even talks to his injured hand.

In one sense, Santiago is defeated by the sharks. His patched sail is "a flag of permanent defeat." But his eyes are "undefeated," and when Manolin comes to see him, they decide to fish together again.

Nature contains this duality as well. It is benevolent and it is harsh. The tuna and dolphin are nourishment to Santiago, but then the sharks come—and the marlin nourishes them.

Why Is *The Old Man and the Sea* a Classic?

There are so many ways to interpret this story, so many things to see in it, but above all there is Santiago—dignified and endearing—a man who persists despite the odds. Hemingway conveys a powerful character and a rich story in spare, simple prose that is layered with meaning. It's the sort of book you can revisit at different times in your life and discover something new with each reading.

Chapter Summary: Fish or Foe

Simple does not have to mean simplistic. In *The Old Man and the Sea*, Hemingway shows us the value of leaving space for the reader to think, allowing the story to hold many interpretations at once. Using the protagonist as an antagonist also creates a strong internal conflict that powers the story forward. In paying careful attention to rhythm, Hemingway incorporates movement into every aspect of the story so that it is more than a motif: it's part of the very structure itself.

Layers of Meaning: Symbols are a literary device in which an object, character, or event represents a deeper, more abstract idea beyond its literal meaning. Symbols act as tangible anchors for abstract concepts, allowing author and reader to explore profound themes through relatable elements within the story.

In *The Old Man and the Sea*, the marlin represents the pursuit of greatness and the honor found in struggle. The sea serves as both a nurturing and an indifferent force, the life-giving and uncontrollable aspects of nature. The lions in Santiago's dreams recall his youth and vitality, the enduring spirit that persists despite physical decline. The sharks signify destruction and the inevitability of loss, both intrinsic to the human experience.

Protagonist as Antagonist: The protagonist is the main character who drives the narrative forward, while the antagonist is the force that opposes the protagonist, creating conflict and obstacles.

Traditionally, these are separate entities—however, when the protagonist and antagonist are the same character, the internal conflict is heightened, centering on the character's personal struggles, flaws, or limitations.

Santiago embodies both roles:

- **As protagonist:** Santiago is the aging fisherman determined to break his unlucky streak by venturing far out to sea to catch a great marlin.

- **As antagonist:** Santiago's greatest obstacles are his own physical limitations, the pains of old age, and his unwavering pride. His internal doubts, exhaustion, and the temptation to surrender all serve as antagonistic forces within himself.

Solitary Protagonist: Crafting scenes—or even entire narratives—with a solitary protagonist poses the challenge of building character and maintaining authenticity without dialogue. Hemingway addresses this by gradually increasing Santiago's self-talk as the conflict intensifies, allowing him to converse with himself, the fish, the warbler, and his own hand.

Giovanni's Room

by James Arthur Baldwin

Internal Conflict Takes Center Stage

In addition to being a novelist, James Arthur Baldwin was also known for his essays, plays, poetry, and social activism. In much of his work, as in his most famous novel, *Go Tell It on the Mountain*, Baldwin writes about the experience of Black Americans facing discrimination and segregation. But when he sent *Giovanni's Room* to his publisher, Knopf rejected the manuscript for straying too far from his previous work. After all, the protagonist, David, is a white American in 1950s Paris struggling to come to terms with his sexuality. But according to Baldwin, "The sexual question and the racial question have always been intertwined." In getting at one, he was critiquing both, and he added in later interviews that he did not want to complicate a story about homophobia with commentary about racism.

That's not to say there isn't racial tension between David and his Italian lover, but the novel's central focus is on David's all-consuming shame about his sexuality. Structurally, the story is very simple: the lovers meet, their chemistry is unquestionable, and the only real obstacle is David's internal struggle. In the end, he leaves Giovanni, thinking he will hate himself less if he commits to a relationship with a woman, but of course that leaves him worse off than ever. What we have here is an unadorned tragic romance. There are no true subplots or side quests, just the simplicity of David's fatal flaw, which leaves us screaming for him to smarten up and accept himself for who he is. Naturally, he doesn't smarten up—and therein lies the emotional draw.

But Baldwin has one more trick up his sleeve to increase the stakes right from the first chapter: the story opens at the end, when everything is at its worst. David's fiancée (now his ex) has left him. And his lover, Giovanni, will soon be executed by guillotine. We don't yet know how the story will reach this point, and so we start out with the promise of a tragic mystery, such that even when the romance is going well, we know that everything will ultimately end badly.

Narrative Goal: The Reluctant Protagonist

Narrative is all about goals and resistance.

As screenwriter Aaron Sorkin said, "I worship at the altar of intention and obstacle. Somebody wants something. Something's standing in their way of getting it. They want the money; they want the girl; they want to get to Philadelphia—doesn't matter. And if they need it, that's even better."

In a traditional narrative (or what the ancient Greek dramaturgists called a comedy), the goal is relatable and deeply personal, such that the reader (or audience) cheers the protagonist toward victory. The alternative, as mentioned in the previous chapter, is the tragic structure. In most tragedies, the protagonist wants something completely stupid. Meanwhile, the reader knows it's stupid, so our emotional draw flows out of cheering for the protagonist to turn their bullshit around and do the right thing.

(A good example of this occurs in *The Picture of Dorian Gray*, which we will analyze in the next chapter.)

In *Giovanni's Room*, this works a bit differently. The protagonist doesn't have a goal that he is working toward. Instead, he is actively resisting a goal. Since it's a romance, David's goal is to fall in love, to reach that *happily ever after* with his boyfriend Giovanni. If he were to actively pursue this goal, the story would be boring, and it would also be over in a few pages. That's because there are no significant external obstacles standing in the way of their relationship. Instead, the obstacle is entirely internal. David is ashamed to be gay, so he thwarts his chances at happiness every step of the way.

PLOT POINTS

Post-Climax Consequences

The story opens at the end. David's fiancée has left him and is on her way from France back to America. His lover Giovanni is awaiting execution. The stakes are set: this isn't going to end well. Starting at this point also creates a mystery, something for the reader to wonder about as the story unfolds: how does it get here?

Fatal Flaw, Misbelief, or Backstory Wound

Often a character's misbelief is revealed slowly. We learn about their skewed perspective or their weakness as we see them mess up over and over again. In *Giovanni's Room,* however, we have a reluctant AND reminiscent narrator, so Baldwin allows us to start with a clear understanding of David's fatal flaw: he is deeply ashamed of being gay.

David's first queer experience was with his best friend Joey back in high school. While their night together was joyous, David couldn't live with himself the next day. He rejected Joey and attempted to reinvent himself with a rougher crowd. He also started drinking and almost died in a car crash. We learn that much of David's shame comes from his father, who low-key suspects his son's sexuality. At one point he overhears his father say, "All I want for David is that he grow up to be a man." He also calls David "Butch" and has no tolerance for femininity. Throughout this backstory overview, the reader can see the truth: David is gay, and no matter how much he tries to suppress it, he's going to be miserable until he can finally accept himself.

Stasis

After high school, David leaves home and seeks to remain in "constant motion," drinking to excess but hating it, with a series of "meaningless" friendships and relationships with women. There's an initial note of misogyny here, with many more to come. David despises what he perceives as his own femininity, so he also disrespects the women in his life. In running from his femininity and sexuality, he ends up in France and, initially, in a relationship with Hella. This whole time, he has avoided having sex with men, but then Hella leaves him to do her own soul-seeking in Spain.

The protagonist's motivation is established in the story's stasis. We know that in his heart David wants to be with men. With Hella gone, his defenses are lowered. He finds himself in the company of other gay men, and there is no one (apart from himself) to judge him for acting on his true desire.

Inciting Incident

David is hanging out with his older friend Jacques at a fancy gay bar. Despite the locale, David is still in full denial mode. He doesn't really like Jacques, whom he brands as a predator of young men, though he borrows money from him, and he also disdains "les folles"—men in the bar who dress in women's clothes and embrace femininity. But then in walks the new barman, Giovanni, for a classic meet-cute moment. David is immediately swooning for this "insolent and dark and leonine" hunk. And Giovanni returns his interest. It's love at first sight, or so it seems. Jacques is a bit annoyed though, in part because he's likewise crushing on Giovanni. David is also warned by a strange man whom he likens to a vampire that he should stay away from the handsome barman or risk great unhappiness. David, however, is overcome with "ferocious excitement." In other words, the protagonist's goal is set. All he must do is get out of his own way. But that turns out to be easier said than done.

Initial Rising Action

Later that night, Jacques issues another warning: he insists that David is lucky to be figuring out who he is at his young age. If he waits until he's older, like Jacques, the struggle will destroy him. His message is simple: quit pretending to be straight. When he commands David to love Giovanni and let this man love him in return, he's not suggesting that they should be together forever, but that they should use the relationship as an opportunity to become their authentic selves.

Once the bar closes, David heads for breakfast with Giovanni, Jacques, and the bar owner, Guillaume. When Giovanni and David have a moment alone, Giovanni introduces a note of foreshadowing: he once slept with Guillaume in exchange for a work permit and a job, and their relationship has been tenuous ever since. Guillaume is another predator who trades favors for sex with desperate young men.

Point of No Return: The Consummation

In a traditional romance, sex often doesn't come right away—it's dangled as a promise or payoff, both for the would-be lovers and the reader. In some cases, there might be an early sex scene, but then the couple is driven apart, such that the reader spends most of the second act yearning for them to get back together. *Giovanni's Room* is not a traditional romance—it's not about courtship but rather about overcoming one's self.

The pair leaves Jacques and Guillaume and returns to Giovanni's small rented room. David is still in denial, but he is overwhelmed by his attraction to Giovanni, which far surpasses anything he ever felt for Hella. His fatal flaw is clear. Just like Jacques, the reader knows what David needs if he is to find happiness.

Rising Action

The relationship enters a brief period of bliss in which we see what the lovers stand to lose. They stay up all night and sleep all day, locked within the safety and privacy of Giovanni's room. Eventually, however, David confesses his relationship with Hella. They have separated but not broken up. Yet his lover isn't concerned. Here too we get some misogyny from Giovanni as he belittles Hella. He also demeans the feminine—in women and in himself. But unlike David, he has come to accept his sexuality and therefore doesn't see Hella as a threat. Readers, on the other hand, know that her return will spell trouble for their relationship.

Months go by. The safety of Giovanni's room evaporates as David comes to hate the small, cramped, and filthy space. The room is at times heaven, but more often it is hell. This is especially true when Giovanni heads out for work, assuming the masculine role and leaving David to wallow in what he sees as feminine dependency.

Midpoint Reversal

David, as noted earlier, is a reluctant protagonist. He rails against himself and seethes with shame. However, he doesn't do anything to change his situation. He doesn't want to change it. He loves Giovanni even as he hates himself for it. Instead, he waits for the world to come along and break the spell.

The midpoint reversal, the point at which the protagonist is forced to take a new path, arrives in the form of two letters. The first is from David's father: he refuses to send any more money to support his son's listless wandering. If there is a woman in his life, David must bring her home. Enough is enough. The second letter is from Hella:

she is done with her soul-searching and will return to Paris in ten days. David's initial reaction is relief. As he hoped, the world has made a decision for him.

Rising Action

In an effort to prepare himself for Hella's arrival, David goes for a long walk, talks to a prostitute, and eventually meets up with an American friend, Sue, whom he seduces. This reignites his shame about his sexuality, and now he dreads Hella's return.

He eventually returns to Giovanni's room to find his lover drunk and angry. When Guillaume, jealous of David, accused his young barman of theft, Giovanni tried to fight him and got fired as a result. David promises to come up with some money, but he makes no attempt to do so. In the days that follow, Giovanni begins chipping away at the bricks in the room. He says he wants to renovate the space and build a bookshelf. He knows the relationship has reached a breaking point; he's trying to give David a reason to stay, as if the room itself is the problem.

Throughout the novel, Giovanni's room is symbolic of their relationship—what starts as a sanctuary quickly turns into a claustrophobic trap, mirroring David's growing internal conflict. Giovanni's desperate attempts to chip away at the bricks are a futile effort to change their reality, but the oppressive atmosphere only deepens their inevitable decline. The room's suffocating walls encapsulate the tragic nature of their love, leaving both characters with nowhere to escape.

Third-Act Spat and False Victory

Another common feature in a traditional romance is the third-act spat—the lovers have a big blowup that seems to dash their chances of ever getting together (or getting back together). In a comedic format, this is usually the all-is-lost plot point. But since

Giovanni's Room is a tragic romance, this fight leads instead to a false victory.

David finally relents and borrows money from Jacques, but when he refers to their apartment as hideous, the tension between him and Giovanni crests and they almost come to blows, each with bricks in hand. "We stared at each other across a narrow space that was full of danger, that almost seemed to roar, like flame." But then they come together, they kiss, and their love is once again intact. However, David still refuses to allow it permanence. "And at moments like this I felt that we were merely enduring and committing the longer and lesser and more perpetual murder."

Tragic Climax

Hella returns to Paris. David redeclares his love for her and proposes marriage. He disappears into her arms for three days and nights, seeking "to drive out fire with fire." On the third day, they run into Giovanni and Jacques, and it's all kinds of awkward. David promises to meet them for a drink later. Afterward, he disparages Giovanni to Hella and agrees that they should soon leave Paris together, but later he softens and even admits to her, "I love him in a way. I really do."

David finally returns to break up with Giovanni. It's at this point that his lover reveals his backstory: he was married to a woman in Italy, but when his son was stillborn, he left. At first, he tries to reason with David, to force him to stop lying to himself, but the fight eventually reaches a plateau. They both know it's over. David spends the night, and in the morning when he gets up to leave, they stare at each other with nothing left to say.

> His body, which I had come to know so well, glowed in the light and charged and thickened the air between us. Then something opened in my brain, a secret, noiseless door swung open, frightening me: it had not occurred to me until

that instant that, in fleeing from his body, I confirmed and perpetuated his body's power over me.

Resolution—the Tragic Consequences

David learns what happens next from Jacques: a letter arrives in a small blue envelope. Giovanni, penniless, tried to get his job back. He presumably slept with Guillaume, who still refused to hire him, after which the ex-barman strangled his ex-boss to death. It wasn't long before Giovanni was captured, confessed, and was sentenced to death.

David and Hella have rented a room in the South of France. He begins to despise her, and when he learns about his ex-lover's fate, he finds himself a sailor and disappears for three days and nights, just as he did to Giovanni. When Hella finds him with the sailor at a gay bar, she confesses that she's always known the truth and breaks off their engagement.

Here the reminiscent narration ends—we've finally caught up with the point in time where the novel began. David is hanging out in the rented room, preparing to leave, agonizing about everything that's led to this point, wallowing in his guilt. He stands before the mirror, cursing his "vile" body, then gets dressed and leaves.

> The morning weighs on my shoulder with the dreaded weight of hope and I take the blue envelope which Jacques had sent to me and tear it slowly into many pieces, watching them dance in the wind, watching the wind carry them away. Yet, as I turn and begin walking toward the waiting people, the wind blows some of them back on me.

Reminiscent Narrator

The reminiscent narrator is a technique we occasionally encounter in the manuscripts we edit in which the narrator speaks from a future point in time. Often, this device is used sporadically and without clear intent, leading to a few common pitfalls. For example, it can undermine tension by assuring readers that the protagonist will survive to tell the tale, thus diluting the stakes of the narrative. Additionally, when the narrator reflects from the future, it can disrupt the reader's immersion in the story's present.

However, Baldwin's use of a reminiscent narrator in *Giovanni's Room* is a textbook example of how this technique can serve a story. From the outset, we know that the romance will end tragically, that David's relationship with Hella is doomed, and that Giovanni will face execution. This knowledge introduces a sense of mystery and heightens the stakes from the beginning. Also, Baldwin primarily uses reminiscent narration as a framing device, allowing the story to unfold in the present tense without constant reminders of the narrator's future perspective. This balance maintains the reader's immersion while also using the future perspective to build intrigue and tension.

Why Is *Giovanni's Room* a Classic?

Giovanni's Room stands out as a classic because it delivers an intense portrayal of internal conflict, masterful dialogue, and brilliant writing overall. Baldwin's characterization captures the raw pain of shame and the struggle for self-acceptance—themes that are, unfortunately, still all too relevant today. Even as society becomes more accepting, homophobia and misogyny persist, leaving many queer kids to grow up in environments where self-loathing is fomented by intolerant parents or communities. David's internalized shame, rooted in his father's toxic expectations, is a reality that still resonates for those grappling with their identity in the face of bigotry and prejudice.

Chapter Summary: An Inside Job

The beauty of *Giovanni's Room* lies in its simplicity. The structure is straightforward, with minimal complications or subplots, yet Baldwin's skillful writing and characterization make it compelling. By creating a reluctant protagonist whose internal conflict serves as the primary obstacle, Baldwin has crafted a story that is as emotionally engaging as it is structurally sound. It's an important reminder that sometimes the most profound narratives are those that explore the human experience with uncomplicated and unflinching honesty.

Reluctant Protagonist: In most narratives, the protagonist has a goal that means a lot to them—that they struggle toward and strive to achieve over the course of the story. However, it's also possible to have a reluctant protagonist who does everything they can to resist their goal. This can create a powerful internal conflict.

Reminiscent Narrator: A reminiscent narrator is one who speaks to the reader from a future point in time, with hindsight and commentary about the actions of the unfolding story. This can be a tricky mode to pull off effectively. It's like broadcasting to readers that the protagonist will get through the current conflict and, in the end, be okay—which can diminish the tension and stakes of the present moment. However, Baldwin uses a reminiscent narrator to great effect in *Giovanni's Room*. By forecasting the coming tragedy, he instills tension in the present moment from page one with the knowledge that this story will end with heartbreak and death.

The Fatal Flaw: Tragic structure is a narrative framework wherein the protagonist possesses a fatal flaw that leads to their inevitable downfall or failure. Unlike traditional (comic) structure, where the protagonist pursues a worthy goal and typically achieves it, tragic structure usually involves the pursuit of a misguided or destructive goal. A fatal flaw is an inherent weakness or misguided belief within a protagonist that leads to their downfall or creates significant obstacles to them achieving their goals. Introducing the fatal flaw early allows readers to understand the character's internal struggles and anticipate the challenges they will face. David's fatal flaw is his deep-seated shame and denial of his own sexuality. This internal conflict prevents him from embracing his true self and sabotages his relationship with Giovanni, ultimately leading to tragic consequences.

The Picture of Dorian Gray

by Oscar Wilde

An Allegory of Good Versus Evil

Oscar Wilde was chiefly known as a playwright and wrote only one novel. While the witticisms in *The Picture of Dorian Gray* showcase his dramatic talents, readers who take his characters (and their clever remarks) at face value will likely become annoyed with the book and might miss the bigger picture. In fact, this novel is a masterful example of how to use both language and characterization to illustrate theme, how to wield showing *and* telling as tools in the service of narrative structure.

Published in 1890, *The Picture of Dorian Gray* is the story of a beautiful young man who unknowingly makes a Faustian bargain to remain eternally youthful. Seems like a good idea. Spoiler alert: it isn't. Like all deals with the devil, the cost is his soul, and the price turns out to be too high.

Few people agree on this novel's genre: it has been categorized as a gothic cautionary tale, horror, a psychological novel, a philosophical novel, and a moral fantasy. In truth, it's all of these things, but what we would call it chiefly is an allegory of good versus evil in the battle for someone's soul.

The story centers on what happens to Dorian after his soul is essentially extracted from the rest of his life and laid out on canvas. But this is also a book about art and morality, the empty pursuit of pleasure for its own sake, the obsession with beauty, and the potential that exists in us all for both good and evil. The name Gray is surely no accident—Dorian becomes a battleground of black versus white.

Dorian Gray is the novel's protagonist, though he shifts at midpoint to become an antihero. Good and evil are represented by the artist Basil Hallward (who sees the best in Dorian) and the dilettante Lord Henry Wotton (who encourages the worst in him) in what amounts to an old-fashioned morality play. At first, the choice seems simple. Basil is pompous and self-righteous and, well, annoying. Lord Henry is more entertaining (though his witticisms become irksome after a while). Evil is seductive, after all. Goodness is a glass of warm milk, and few people are willing to upset the balance of their life in pursuit of that.

Narrative Goal

As we saw in *Giovanni's Room*, in a tragedy the action is driven more by the protagonist's fatal flaw than by a relatable goal. But in this case, the reader can see that the protagonist's goal is not worth achieving and should not be achieved. Instead, we root for the protagonist to overcome their fatal flaw and realize they must give up on the narrative goal.

When we examine Dorian's narrative goal, here's what we find:

When Dorian sees the portrait Basil has painted of him, he falls in love with it and wishes he could remain eternally youthful and let the portrait age instead. Not realizing he is a pawn in a moral tug-of-war, his wish instantly comes true. Dorian is now free to pursue pleasure without moral restraint; his portrait will suffer the consequences of vice while he remains both young and innocent looking. He believes it's a foolproof plan, but as his hedonistic lifestyle spins out of control, the reader senses the impending disaster. Will he succeed in reimposing moral restraint on his life (getting what he needs), or will he finally reap what he has sown (getting what he deserves)?

In other words, will good or evil triumph in this allegory?

PLOT POINTS

Stasis and Inciting Incident

The novel begins as a morality play with the face-off of good versus evil before the unsuspecting victim walks onstage. The setting is Edenic, and good and evil are clearly defined. Readers meet a bombastic artist spouting a lot of high-minded philosophy on the nature of both art and beauty to his rakish friend, who makes one witty remark after the next and shreds a daisy to bits.

The first time we read this, we thought *where was the editor?* How could they have allowed *this* to be the beginning of the novel? It's not an easy entry point. Other people we spoke to who tried to read the novel put it down in the middle of this stasis scene because they Just. Couldn't. Take it. But as soon as we realized this was an allegory and that these two men—angel and devil—were fighting over Dorian's soul, we understood the novel couldn't start anywhere *but* here.

When the story opens, Basil has already painted Dorian's portrait a number of times and is praising him to Lord Henry. Indeed, it seems Basil has fallen in love with Dorian. When Lord Henry sees the beauty and innocence in the picture, his spidey senses go wild. Here is the perfect man to corrupt. Basil realizes it would be a very bad thing for Lord Henry and Dorian to meet. Lord Henry would ruin him. He decides this must not happen... and then a servant announces Dorian Gray is at the door.

But Basil hasn't painted THE picture yet. That happens now, and it forms the inciting incident. Dorian enters the story as an innocent:

"One felt that he had kept himself unspotted from the world." He's not interested in having a life-sized portrait done of him and pays little attention to his appearance... until he agrees to sit for Basil one more time and Lord Henry starts talking to him.

Henry encourages a life of the senses as a path to self-realization: "The only way to get rid of temptation is to yield to it." To indulge in pleasure without moral restraint. When he says this, there's a change on Dorian's face, which Basil captures on the canvas. This is the moment when his narrative goal takes shape. The devil has spoken, and his victim has listened—but he has not fallen. Yet.

The Point of No Return

While Basil paints, Dorian goes out into the garden, where Henry talks about the importance of youth and the withering effects of time. Dorian realizes the painting will retain his youthful beauty, but he will not. Henry spies his chance: "There is absolutely nothing in the world but youth!" he says and warns Dorian of how the world judges by appearance.

At last, the portrait is finished, and it is Basil's masterpiece. When Dorian sees it, he falls in love with his own image in a classic Narcissus moment and bemoans the passage of time: "How sad it is! I shall grow old, and horrible, and dreadful. But this picture will remain always young ... If it were only the other way! If it were I who was to be always young, and the picture that was to grow old! ... I would give my soul for that!"

As soon as he says this, he has unwittingly crossed the point of no return. He gets what he wants, which is a significant step toward his narrative goal. He can indulge in pleasure without moral restraint (and, he believes, without consequence). The question then becomes whether he *will* indulge himself unrestrainedly, and if so, what will happen to him? Will he survive the fallout, or is he doomed to self-destruction? Will Dorian conquer temptation, as

Lord Henry has suggested? This fits the tragic structure because it will drive Dorian toward a goal the reader doesn't actually want him to achieve (since we know it will end badly).

Seeing the effect of his work, Basil immediately wants to destroy it, but Dorian won't let him. Instead, Basil sends the portrait home with Dorian, speaking of it as if it were a person. Henry, too, refers to two Dorians—the one standing before him and the one in the portrait. But neither Dorian nor the reader realizes yet the terrible bargain he has made. By the end of this scene, Dorian chooses to go to the theater with Henry rather than dining with Basil: and so, another choice has been made.

Rising Action

Lord Henry continues to influence Dorian with his clever speeches, extolling the virtues of selfishness and the pursuit of pleasure. Meanwhile, Dorian wanders into a theater in a poor neighborhood and falls in love with the actress Sibyl Vane.

Sibyl knows him only as Prince Charming and adores him. Her brother James, however, is suspicious of Dorian's intentions. James is about to leave for Australia, but he warns both Sibyl and their mother that if "Prince Charming" does anything to harm Sibyl, he will track him down and kill him.

When Dorian declares his intention to marry Sibyl, Henry ridicules him and Basil can't control his feelings of jealousy. Love seems to be the one thing powerful enough to conquer Henry's influence. Dorian drags Basil and Henry to one of Sibyl's performances, having praised her marvelous acting talents, but Sibyl delivers a terrible performance and Dorian is mortified. She explains afterward that meeting him made her realize everything she did onstage was fake—in essence, that love is more important than art. She intends to give up acting and devote herself to him instead. Dorian realizes he was only in love with her acting and breaks up with her.

At home, he notices there's a look of cruelty in the portrait that wasn't there before. He has an epiphany about his character and realizes he treated Sibyl badly and that Lord Henry is not a good influence on him. He doesn't want to become the man in the portrait. The allegorical battle of good versus evil is now playing out within him. There is still enough residual goodness inside him to form an obstacle to the other part of him that is committed to hedonism. He resolves to marry Sibyl and become a good human being. He will not see Lord Henry anymore.

Here Wilde uses the reader's vain hope that Dorian's realization of his mistake will stick.

Our emotional draw is fueled by our desire for Dorian to give up on his goal of unbridled hedonism rather than pressing on (as opposed to how we root for the protagonist to achieve their goal in a comic structure).

It almost happens. But by the time Dorian makes this decision, it's too late: Sibyl has already committed suicide.

Midpoint Reversal

Sibyl's death marks a shift in Dorian from the self-love of Narcissus to self-hatred, and from protagonist to antihero. The internal war of good versus evil shifts as well. Before the midpoint, the force of goodness had the upper hand. After the midpoint, Dorian fights against it. He fully embraces the hedonism Lord Henry has been advocating all along and makes a conscious decision to be a witness to his own moral demise. After all, the portrait will bear the brunt of it, not him.

Basil comes to comfort Dorian after Sibyl's death and is shocked to find that he went to the opera that night with Henry. Basil says he wants to exhibit the portrait, but Dorian refuses to let him see it now that it has changed. There's an important shift in their relationship.

Basil notices that Dorian is different. Dorian, who had once been aligned with Basil, is now firmly in Henry's camp. Henry gives him a mysterious yellow book that guides him into the world of decadence and immorality. Critics believe this was *À rebours* by Joris-Karl Huysmans, a Parisian book that influenced British aesthetes and was wrapped in yellow paper as a warning for its X-rated content.

Now that Dorian realizes all his secret vices are evident on the portrait's face, he must keep it hidden or else people will find out the truth about him—that his outward appearance is a lie, and his soul is ugly. He locks the portrait in an unused room and embraces his dark side, believing that if no one can see the effects of his behavior, then it doesn't matter.

Rising Action

Eighteen years pass. As Dorian descends further into a life of debauchery, he becomes fascinated by the contrast between his facade of purity and the evil and cruelty of his soul as reflected in the portrait. For a time, the writing shifts from scene to summary as Dorian devotes himself to beauty for its own sake: jewels, perfumes, tapestries, embroidery. It is, in fact, art for art's sake. There is no longer anything creative about it. The writing becomes informational, trivial, boring. It doesn't reveal character. It's all about *stuff*, and about people with titles whom we don't know and don't care about. It's superficial and loses all meaning, just like Dorian's soulless life. Wilde is showing us that a life without time or consequences is meaningless.

Basil comes to visit Dorian before a planned trip to Paris and tells him there are terrible rumors going around about his bad behavior, that sin is never secret—it "writes itself across a man's face." But for Dorian, this isn't true. His sins are only evident in the portrait. While Basil might be a bit pompous, he is the book's moral compass, and he genuinely cares for Dorian. He appears here as a possible savior.

When Basil voices a wish to see Dorian's soul, Dorian shows him the painting. Basil is horrified. While he still believes it's possible to redeem Dorian, Dorian says it's too late. In a fit of rage, Dorian blames Basil for everything that has happened and kills him. He then calls on an old friend and chemist, Alan Campbell, to dispose of the body in a way that all fans of *Breaking Bad* will recognize. Campbell at first refuses, but Dorian threatens to blackmail him by exposing some secret of his. We never find out what it is, but the reader assumes it involves something sexual.

Dorian has progressed from corruption to crime. The painting now shows blood dripping from one hand, a nice gothic touch.

False Victory

After Basil's murder, Dorian falls apart. Hanging out with Lord Henry doesn't make him feel better, so he heads to the opium dens. While there, he runs into a man whose drug addiction Dorian is partly responsible for—and even though he makes excuses for his responsibility, his conscience is awakened (so he's *not* irredeemable after all—another bit of false hope planted by Wilde). The consequences of his actions might not be evident on his own face, but he is surrounded by the destruction that he has caused.

When a woman refers to him as Prince Charming, Sibyl's brother James happens to be there and overhears. Yes, nice coincidence—but at least it gets Dorian into more trouble rather than less. James never knew Dorian's real name, but he's been hunting him for years. He attacks him, but Dorian is saved by his youthful appearance. Sibyl's death was eighteen years ago. Dorian couldn't possibly have caused it—look how young he is. But after Dorian leaves, the woman who spoke earlier assures James that Dorian has been coming there for eighteen years, and in all that time he has never aged a day.

Dorian is pursued by his conscience in the form of James, whom he imagines seeing everywhere. During a hunting trip, when one of his friends is about to shoot a hare, Dorian tries to stop him and is horrified when a man hiding in the brush is shot and killed by accident—and it just so happens to be James.

Dorian has literally dodged a bullet and believes he has been spared some terrible fate. This represents a false victory. Once again, he has not gotten what he deserves—a point that definitely plays into his downfall. He is repeatedly spared from both conscience and karma, and yet, is he? There's only one thing worse than getting caught: not getting caught.

Tragic Climax

Determined to clean up his life, Dorian meets a village girl and resists the opportunity to defile her. Lord Henry ridicules him for this, but it now sounds pretty empty. When Dorian goes to check the painting, hoping that his one decent act of sparing the girl has had an effect on it, all he sees in the face is hypocrisy. The consequences of his actions are accruing. Alan Campbell, the man he blackmailed to dispose of Basil's body, has committed suicide.

Tragic climaxes typically end in catastrophe—the final consequence of the protagonist's fatal flaw. Up to this point, Dorian has gotten what he wanted (to behave with impunity and allow the painting to age instead of him), but he realizes at the end that the cost is too high, and he can no longer live with it. Sins that go unpunished are a terrible thing. Youth and beauty have ruined him. His conscience has risen up with full power, and he can no longer resist it. He smashes the mirror Lord Henry gave him (a great symbolic gesture, given the earlier Narcissus vibes).

When Dorian realizes the painting is evidence against him, he takes the knife he used to stab Basil and tries to destroy it. But because the painting contains his soul, this amounts to suicide. The novel resolves with the discovery of his dead body and a painting on the wall of the young Dorian as he looked when he first sat for Basil.

Everything Is Purposeful

In the beginning of the novel, Basil's high-minded bombast seems to grate on purpose, while Lord Henry's cleverness is more appealing. Evil is, after all, a temptation. Goodness requires effort. But as the novel proceeds, these two characters experience reversals. Basil starts to make more sense.

His concern for Dorian's well-being is sincere whereas Lord Henry soon seems merely manipulative. His superficiality is reflected in Dorian's new lifestyle: those long paragraphs about jewels and embroidery and perfume are written in such a way as to make them *feel* superficial. In general, summary-mode narration tends to break reader immersion, but Wilde intentionally uses summary to demonstrate theme. He drops meaningless names to show us the meaninglessness of name-dropping. He shows the emptiness of a life based only on the pursuit of pleasure for its own sake.

Lord Henry's cleverness eventually rings false, especially as we see Dorian's moral decay and the ruin of anyone who comes into contact with him.

Why Is *The Picture of Dorian Gray* a Classic?

Any novel that forces the reader to think long after they've finished it is one that will stand up to several readings. As a bonus, a writer who wants to understand the principles of showing versus telling can't do better than to dissect this novel.

In terms of themes, the desire for eternal youth never seems to go out of style (hello Instagram, Vogue, and about ten thousand other things that make up our present-day society). Wilde would be pleased—and perhaps disappointed—to know how relevant his novel is to today's readers. It has a surprising amount to say about our narcissistic selfie society and the social media personas we project to the world, when the truth is often so different.

Chapter Summary: Shades of Gray

Oscar Wilde makes effective use of allegory combined with just the right amount of gothic to produce a haunting tale with a terrific midpoint reversal. If you want to understand tragic structure, *The Picture of Dorian Gray* is a great example.

Everything in this novel is intentional (as it should be in every novel). When you're tempted to ask yourself *why on earth did the author do that?* it behooves you to dig for the answer—because there always is one. No choice is random or accidental. That is the level of care we must take with our work.

Midpoints and Reversals: As previously mentioned, a midpoint serves to raise the stakes, deepen the conflict, or shift the direction of the narrative. Midpoints can take various forms:

- **Mini-climax:** A significant event that heightens tension but doesn't resolve the main conflict.
- **Thematic shift:** A change in the story's focus or the introduction of new themes.
- **Major obstacle:** A new challenge that significantly complicates the protagonist's journey.
- **Reversal:** A dramatic change in the protagonist's narrative goal that completely alters the story's trajectory.

A reversal involves a significant shift but doesn't always occur at the midpoint; it can happen at any point in the story, and there can be multiple reversals. Conversely, while the midpoint is a singular event in the narrative structure, it isn't always characterized by a reversal. In *The Picture of Dorian Gray*, the midpoint functions as a reversal. The suicide of Sibyl Vane marks this pivotal moment. Prior to her death, Dorian harbors the possibility of redemption; afterward, he succumbs to the evil within him.

Coincidences in Fiction: Coincidences in storytelling are a double-edged sword. In real life, they astonish us because of their sheer improbability. However, in fiction, coincidences can feel contrived because readers are acutely aware that the author orchestrates every event. This is especially true when a coincidence conveniently aids the protagonist. Positive coincidences that solve problems or advance the hero's quest can undermine tension and make the narrative seem lazy. They can also cause the reader to lose faith in the story.

That said, coincidences aren't entirely taboo in fiction. They can be (very occasionally) effective, especially when they introduce a new obstacle or complication for the protagonist—a negative coincidence. Coincidences also work well as inciting incidents—such as a chance event that disrupts the protagonist's normal life and sets the narrative in motion.

In *The Picture of Dorian Gray*, Oscar Wilde employs a negative coincidence when James Vane, the brother of Dorian's former fiancée Sibyl, overhears someone refer to Dorian as "Prince Charming" in an opium den. James has been searching for the man who wronged his sister, and this chance encounter reignites his quest for vengeance. This coincidence doesn't aid Dorian; instead, it introduces a new threat that escalates the tension and forces Dorian to confront the consequences of his actions.

Summary-Mode Narration: Summary is the opposite of scene. While scene is the dramatization of a focal character's moment-to-moment experience, summary pauses the experience to explain. Summary can be useful for moving your protagonist between locales or zipping ahead in time, but excessive summary lacks the vividness and immediacy that is crucial to reader immersion.

Wilde intentionally uses summary mode to reflect the emptiness of Dorian's hedonistic lifestyle following his moral decline. After the pivotal midpoint where Dorian fully embraces a life of indulgence, the narrative shifts into long passages that catalog his obsessions with jewels, music, tapestries, and other luxuries. These summaries lack the immersive quality of scenes and instead provide a detached overview of his pursuits.

This narrative choice serves a thematic purpose. By presenting Dorian's activities in summary, Wilde emphasizes the superficiality and monotony of his existence. The lack of detailed scenes mirrors the lack of depth in Dorian's experiences. In essence, Wilde is rendering the emptiness of a life devoted solely to aesthetic pleasures without moral grounding. In other words, he's boring us *on purpose*.

Pride and Prejudice

by Jane Austen

First Impressions

Arguably Jane Austen's most popular novel, *Pride and Prejudice* hits all the high points of the romance arc—and is considered by many to be foundational to that genre. Austen builds each protagonist's trials into the narrative structure in a nicely symmetrical fashion before and after the midpoint. What's interesting about this novel in terms of craft is how she experiments with free indirect discourse within the omniscient point of view (don't worry, we'll explain).

Also notable is her frank portrayal of a woman's plight in nineteenth-century England. When it came to marriage, love was a luxury that not many women could afford. Austen juxtaposes the hope of finding true love with the reality of marrying for financial security—all set against a backdrop of a highly classed society.

Satire plays a key role in this novel. Austen was not the first to wield this sword against the upper classes, but she does it with such wit and cleverness that it's a delight to read.

Pride and Prejudice is an examination of human nature, particularly the danger of making assumptions about a person based on appearances. Interestingly, its original title was *First Impressions*, which is reflected in how several of the characters judge each other too hastily. The main characters—Elizabeth Bennet and Mr. Darcy—are particularly guilty of this. Not only do they misjudge each other, but Elizabeth also misjudges Mr. Wickham, and Mr. Darcy misjudges

Jane. The pride and prejudice that both Darcy and Elizabeth bring into their assumptions almost keep them apart forever.

But fear not. This is a romance—*happily ever after* is part of the deal.

Narrative Goal

The novel's opening line is so well-known, it comes up in trivia games: "It is a truth universally acknowledged, that a single man in possession of a good fortune, must be in want of a wife."

In fact, this novel is about the exact opposite of that statement: the truth that is not acknowledged. A single woman who is not in possession of a good fortune had better hunt for a rich husband or she'll be in trouble. And a single man in possession of a good fortune will be bound by family and societal expectations to only look for a certain type of woman (i.e., a wealthy one).

This is an ugly truth, and Austen creates an ugly character to express it: Mrs. Bennet. Mrs. Bennet is loud and lacks social graces and connives to do whatever she can to find partners for her daughters. But though we might dislike her, we cannot deny that she sees reality more clearly than most. With five daughters and the family estate entailed to a distant male cousin, Mrs. Bennet understands the transactional nature of marriage for a woman. She herself has no inheritance, so when Mr. Bennet dies, if one of the daughters is not married to a man *in possession of a good fortune* who can support them, they'll be destitute.

But what about love? Jane and Elizabeth (the two eldest daughters) are looking for true love, Mary (the middle child) is up to her neck in books, and Lydia and Kitty (the youngest) are flighty and silly. It is worth pointing out the irony that Mr. and Mrs. Bennet do not have a happy marriage. He scarcely tolerates her and sequesters himself in his library so that he doesn't have to listen to her. They are an object lesson to their daughters of the dangers of marrying too impulsively.

If the narrative structure were expressed in Mrs. Bennet's terms, it would look thus: when an eligible bachelor rolls into town, Mrs. Bennet is determined to match him up with one of her daughters, else her girls will end up penniless.

While that goal underpins the whole novel, Mrs. Bennet is not one of the protagonists. The two key protagonists are Elizabeth Bennet and Mr. Darcy, and while this is a love story, it takes two-thirds of the novel before their emotions are in sync and the final third before they can overcome the various obstacles that keep them apart.

Since there are two protagonists, we will examine both arcs.

Darcy's is as follows: when a wealthy man falls in love with a woman from a middle-class family, he must overcome his societal prejudices or else he'll be stuck marrying the insipid daughter of his powerful aunt.

And Elizabeth's: when a young woman's pride is injured by a wealthy eligible bachelor, she makes faulty assumptions about his character and must eventually swallow her pride and forgive him—else she will remain unmarried and potentially destitute.

PLOT POINTS

Because *Pride and Prejudice* sets the foundation for the genre of romance, it seems fitting to evaluate its structure based on what has become the formula for many romance novels. Though Austen's novel includes all the main structural elements of a romance, it doesn't quite hit them in the order readers have come to expect. But they're still there.

Stasis

Stasis serves as the foundation for protagonist motivation. This is where generalized desire already exists, so that when the inciting incident happens and a specific narrative goal is formed, it is perceived to come from *somewhere*.

The opening of the novel sets up the social context and shows us this generalized desire. We meet the Bennets, a middle-class family with five unmarried daughters living in the village of Longbourn on an estate that is entailed to a cousin. Those daughters must get married, and soon.

When Mr. Bingley arrives in town and rents Netherfield Park, we have the narrative hook: an eligible bachelor who is wealthy to boot. He must marry *someone*, and Mrs. Bennet is determined it will be one of her daughters.

Inciting Incident (Initial Encounter)

The ball in Meryton is the inciting incident for the two main love stories in the novel. It is the initial encounter for both Jane and Mr. Bingley, and Elizabeth and Mr. Darcy, bringing us a meet-cute moment and a rejection.

When Mr. Bingley sets eyes on Jane, it is love at first sight for them both. He has come to the ball with his good friend, Mr. Darcy. While Bingley seems to get along with everyone, the same cannot be said for Darcy, who comes across as proud and haughty. Bingley suggests that he might dance with Jane's sister, Elizabeth, but Darcy refuses, calling Elizabeth merely "tolerable" and "not handsome enough" to tempt him.

The First Rejection

Unfortunately, Elizabeth overhears this statement. In contrast to the love at first sight that Jane and Bingley experience, for Darcy and

Elizabeth it is more like disdain at first sight. When Elizabeth vows to her best friend Charlotte that she will never dance with Mr. Darcy or have anything to do with him because he's too proud and disagreeable, the seeds of pride and prejudice are planted for them both. Darcy appears to be proud; Elizabeth's pride has been injured. Darcy is prejudiced against Elizabeth's lower standing in society; Elizabeth judges Darcy based on her first impression of him, which will turn out to be wrong. It's a moment of mutual rejection.

Initial Rising Action

In a romance cycle, the two main characters have conflicting intentions for the relationship. The rising action involves them challenging or reinforcing these positions through three trials. Austen uses the three trials in a slightly different way, separating them out and creating symmetry around the midpoint. Let's look at the key initial events first as they relate to Darcy and Elizabeth and then move into the trials.

Jane is invited to Netherfield Park to dine with Mr. Bingley's sister, Caroline. Mrs. Bennet, ever mindful of snagging the eligible bachelor, forces Jane to go on horseback in the rain so that she will get sick and have to stay there to convalesce. This has an unintended consequence: Elizabeth goes to visit Jane, and during that time, Mr. Darcy begins to fall in love with her.

But Darcy also watches Jane and misreads her reserved nature toward Bingley as disinterest. He cautions his friend against pursuing the relationship (though Elizabeth doesn't know this yet). Elizabeth's opinion of Darcy worsens when she meets Mr. Wickham, who tells her that Darcy cheated him out of his inheritance.

At Rosings Park, Darcy attempts to connect with Elizabeth and explains that he doesn't have the easy ability to converse with strangers, which is why he comes across as standoffish, but when

Elizabeth learns that he convinced Bingley not to pursue her sister, she is enraged.

The Midpoint Declaration

Darcy declares his love for Elizabeth, but he does it in an awkward and almost insulting way, telling her that he loves her despite his better judgment and her poor relations. Elizabeth refuses him, partly because she doesn't appreciate how he's expressed himself, but mainly because of what he's done to her sister and what she's learned about him from Wickham. Her rejection of him couldn't be stronger: she wouldn't marry him if he were the last man on earth.

And yet, as soon as he storms out, she bursts into tears—suggesting that she has developed feelings for him too. But it now seems that the distance between them is unbridgeable. Shortly after the declaration, Darcy delivers a letter, which becomes the turning point in the novel. The scales fall from Elizabeth's eyes, and she begins to form a different opinion of him. He must humble himself to write this letter, and Elizabeth must humble herself to accept how wrong she was about his character. Transformation has begun.

Three Trials

In the romance genre, these three trials usually involve the would-be lovers becoming closer while also reinforcing why the relationship can't work. In the case of a romance with another external conflict, the would-be lovers must work through their own rising action in three trials that bring them into contact with each other and build on the initial rejection. Sometimes the trials take the form of three dates. That's not quite what Austen does here, though both Elizabeth and Darcy experience three distinct trials.

Elizabeth's trials happen before the midpoint and make up most of the rising action in the first half of the book. They come in the form of suitors:

- Mr. Collins: the cousin who is destined to inherit the family estate but who is wholly unsuitable for her. This marriage would be prudent financially, but unhappy.
- Mr. Wickham: a charming militia officer who turns out to be a scoundrel. This marriage would be based on physical attraction and would be a disaster.
- Mr. Darcy: the perfect partner, whom Elizabeth hates at first and who is, in terms of class, out of her league. This marriage would be ideal, but societal expectation (represented by Lady Catherine de Bourgh) is against it.

Darcy's trials happen after his midpoint declaration of love for Elizabeth. Because they make up the bulk of the rising action in the second half of the book, they overlap with the external crisis. They come in the form of amends:

- He writes a long letter of explanation about what happened with Mr. Bingley and Jane, admitting he was wrong in his assumptions of her. He also explains the truth about Mr. Wickham—who, it turns out, is unreliable, immoral, and had nefarious designs on Darcy's sister Georgiana (and specifically, her fortune).
- He secretly helps with Lydia's situation when she and Mr. Wickham run away together.
- He returns to Longbourn with Mr. Bingley to right the wrong of having thwarted his relationship with Jane.

While Elizabeth and Darcy don't exactly declare their love for each other yet, it is clear that she has been affected by his letter and that he's not prepared to give up on her.

External Crisis: All Is Lost

The external crisis comes when Elizabeth receives news that Lydia and Mr. Wickham have run away together to elope and that they are traveling alone (and possibly still unmarried).

It's important to understand how serious this was. A young girl's reputation was everything; losing it would impact not only her but also her entire family. While Austen spends a lot of time making fun of social hierarchy, this part of the novel is deadly serious. No honorable man would marry the sister of such a disreputable girl.

Because Darcy is present when Elizabeth receives this news, she shares it with him. Their reactions are an indication of how much they've both changed. Elizabeth feels at least partly responsible because she knew about Wickham's true character but never said anything to her family. Darcy, too, takes responsibility, saying that he should have exposed Wickham publicly.

Mr. Bennet and Mr. Gardiner are dispatched to track Lydia down in London, where she is presumed to be holed up with Mr. Wickham. But there is little hope of finding them, and even less hope that Mr. Wickham will do the right thing and marry her—especially because she has no money.

This is an all-is-lost moment for Elizabeth. Her feelings for Darcy have now come full circle, and she would marry him if he asked. But she now believes there's no chance of him doing so with a sister whose reputation is so wholly ruined.

What no one realizes is that Darcy is working behind the scenes to remedy the situation. This is part of his second trial.

Pulling Together

Pulling together involves the couple's response to the crisis, but because Austen weaves Darcy's trials into the fabric of the later rising action, the causality here belongs to him.

Despite the odds, Lydia and Wickham are found and return to Longbourn as a married couple. Lydia lets it slip that Mr. Darcy was at their wedding. When Elizabeth questions her aunt about it, she discovers it was Darcy who saved her sister. He was the one who paid Wickham's debts and offered him enough money to make marrying Lydia an attractive option. For Darcy to go out of his way to help Wickham after everything Wickham has done to him and his sister is a remarkable gesture of love to Elizabeth.

The characters of Wickham and Mr. Darcy are set up as opposites. Wickham is good-looking and charming and has good social skills, while Darcy seems haughty and awkward and is unable to communicate well. But this novel is at least partly about appearances being deceptive. Darcy turns out to be irreproachable while Wickham is a rogue who is not to be trusted.

Darcy's third trial occurs when he arrives at Longbourn with Mr. Bingley to correct his earlier mistake.

Climax

It almost seems like things will work out for Elizabeth and Mr. Darcy, until Lady Catherine de Bourgh pays the Bennets a surprise visit. Throughout the novel she has attempted to exert control over everyone around her, and as a wealthy patroness, she expects people to do her bidding.

Austen introduces a lovely irony into this climax. It is Catherine de Bourgh's attempt to end the relationship between Darcy and Elizabeth that brings them together. She has heard a rumor that Darcy and Elizabeth are engaged and insists on Elizabeth promising never to enter into such an arrangement. Elizabeth refuses. When Lady Catherine relates this refusal to Darcy, he realizes he still has a chance with her. This is what spurs him to propose to her a second time. This time, she accepts.

The HEA—Happily Ever After

Jane and Mr. Bingley marry. Elizabeth and Darcy marry. Lydia and Mr. Wickham have a rocky marriage, which is pretty much what they deserve. Kitty spends more time with Elizabeth and Darcy and is thus elevated from being Lydia's silly, irresponsible sister to a more thoughtful and well-mannered young lady.

The only person who doesn't get what they deserve is poor Mary, who really would have been the perfect partner for Mr. Collins.

Free Indirect Discourse

Jane Austen's experimentation with free indirect discourse was something new in the literary world. Free indirect discourse is basically a mash-up of the objectivity of omniscient narration with the intimacy of deep third. It means taking away the filtering phrases (*she thought*) and allowing a character's thoughts to simply exist on the page. The resulting prose flows more smoothly and affords the reader a more direct experience of the characters.

It's important to differentiate this from head hopping, which involves quick (and confusing) shifts in POV. In free indirect discourse, the characters' perspectives are filtered through the narrator's voice. It allows for a more immersive experience than the omniscient narration that was typical of the time.

Why Is *Pride and Prejudice* a Classic?

Jane Austen certainly wasn't the first author to think about writing a story in which romance figures prominently as a literary theme. Before her there was *Romeo and Juliet*, *Cinderella*, and all those troubadours with their love poems. But *Pride and Prejudice* is foundational to the development of the romance genre in the way it establishes some important elements that have become so popular they are now considered tropes: the meet-cute moment, the enemies-to-lovers transformation, the opposites-attract idea, and of course, the happily-ever-after ending. Romance is not relegated to a subplot; it is the plot.

Pride and Prejudice also distinguishes itself for its frank look at women's financial and societal circumstances in nineteenth-century England. It offers commentary on class differences, the ridiculous expectations and behaviors of the very wealthy, and the unfair inheritance laws. It's a novel that stands up to repeated reading and never ceases to be both relevant and entertaining, proving that simple domestic stories are as engaging and valuable as sweeping epics.

Chapter Summary: Hearts and Hubris

In *Pride and Prejudice*, Austen gives us nuanced characters, witty dialogue, unexpected plot twists, and characters who transform in important ways. The narrative structure provides readers with a dynamic and satisfying romance in the relationship between Darcy and Elizabeth. Both protagonists get clearly defined arcs, and Austen creates a satisfying balance in the mirroring of three trials apiece.

The Structure of a Romance: The romance genre typically follows some key plot points: an initial meeting (sometimes called a meet-cute), initial attraction and rejection, coming together, three dates (or three trials), midpoint kiss and crisis, coming back together, the fall (breakup), the sacrifice and declaration, and finally a resolution leading to a happily ever after (HEA). In *Pride and Prejudice*, Austen gives us an early form of this structure through the evolving relationship between Elizabeth and Darcy.

Enemies to Lovers: The enemies-to-lovers trope involves characters who start out with animosity or a misunderstanding but gradually develop romantic feelings for each other. This dynamic is appealing because it builds tension and allows for significant character growth as the would-be lovers overcome their differences. In *Pride and Prejudice*, Elizabeth and Darcy embody this trope. Their initial rejection evolves into respect and love as they confront their own flaws and learn more about each other. Their journey illustrates the *opposites-attract* concept, making their eventual union deeply satisfying.

Three Trials: In romance narratives, the three trials or dates are a series of interactions that bring the protagonists closer while testing their relationship. These events challenge their perceptions and contribute to character development.

Happily Ever After (HEA): The happily-ever-after ending is a defining element of the romance genre, providing a satisfying conclusion where the protagonists overcome obstacles to be together. It fulfills the reader's expectation for a positive resolution. In *Pride and Prejudice*, the HEA is achieved when Elizabeth and Darcy both overcome their pride and prejudices. They recognize their faults, forgive each other, and unite in marriage. Their union not only brings personal happiness but also reconciles family tensions and societal expectations.

Free Indirect Discourse: Free indirect discourse is a narrative technique that blends the character's thoughts and feelings with otherwise omniscient third-person narration without explicit indicators like "she thought" or "he wondered." It allows readers to access a character's inner world seamlessly while maintaining the narrative voice.

Of Mice and Men

by John Steinbeck

The Best Laid Schemes

Published in 1937, John Steinbeck's novella, *Of Mice and Men*, is a masterpiece of foreshadowing and an object lesson in how to use cohesive imagery to serve both narrative structure and theme. It is one of the few longer works of fiction that employs the objective point of view, which is remarkably effective in allowing readers to think for themselves about what Steinbeck is doing and why. (An objective POV presents events and characters without internal thoughts or feelings, compelling readers to infer motivations and emotions from actions and dialogue alone.) The narrative structure is efficient and clean.

The novella is also surprisingly controversial—frequently banned, even in 2024—and is on the American Library Association's list of the top 100 banned books. Which proves yet again that some people just don't understand the point of reading fiction.

The title comes from Robert Burns' poem, "To A Mouse": "The best laid schemes o' Mice an' Men…" fall apart, and instead of joy, we get "grief an' pain." But *Of Mice and Men* is about far more than plans falling through. It explores the relationship between humanity and the animal world and what happens when humans are treated like animals.

This heartbreaking novella is about what it means to be human.

Narrative Goal

Of Mice and Men takes place during the Great Depression near Soledad, California, and tells the story of two migrant workers, George Milton and Lennie Small. George, the protagonist, is quick-witted, pragmatic, and street-smart. He has teamed up with Lennie, who has significant challenges with understanding and processing information. Other characters are immediately suspicious of their friendship; they assume George must want something from Lennie. Why else would he hang out with him?

The thing is, Lennie offers companionship. The mark of a person's character is their willingness to help others while expecting nothing in return, and while George sometimes complains about taking care of Lennie, it's obvious that he cares deeply for him and is protective of him. Lennie has certain stories that he repeats like mantras, and one of them is about friendship and how he and George are different from the typical ranch hands who battle loneliness: "I got you to look after me, and you got me to look after you..."

Their companionship becomes a dynamic theme. The characters who are vulnerable—like Candy and Crooks—see the value in it and want to join in. The theme of companionship is linked to George and Lennie's shared goal, which is to own a ranch—which really amounts to reclaiming their dignity. They want a place of their own where they call the shots, raise their own animals, and grow their own food—where they "live off the fat of the land," as Lennie puts it, which seems like an impossible dream during the Great Depression.

This is the underlying stasis motivation and the source of the long-term stakes. George has secured jobs on a new ranch so that they can save the money they need to purchase some land. But George's real job on this ranch is to safeguard Lennie. That is his narrative goal. Lennie is big and doesn't know his own strength. He also tends to say and do things that are misconstrued as inappropriate. Lennie's sole focus is on the future ranch, specifically on taking care of the rabbits. That's all he thinks about.

To express the narrative structure in formal terms: When Lennie has an incident with a woman, he and George have to run away and get new jobs. But when Curley and his flirtatious young wife show up, George must keep Lennie out of trouble or else they will never get their ranch.

This also creates an internal conflict for George because he doesn't want to be alone. He teams up with Lennie because this gives him someone to care about. Caring for Lennie is what makes him human. He must protect Lennie or else something terrible will happen to him, and then George will end up not only alone but also less than human.

PLOT POINTS

In Medias Res

Steinbeck starts by using imagery in an intentional way. The novella is bookended by a riverside scene that, in the beginning, is pastoral. Steinbeck also describes Lennie with animal characteristics, like a bear. Both elements become important later.

The novella begins after the inciting incident has already happened. Because Lennie forgets day-to-day details, he is in the same position as the reader in terms of lacking context. This allows Steinbeck to fill in the gaps of both stasis and the inciting incident because George has to keep reminding Lennie of what they're doing (going to a new job) and why (because they had to run away from the last one in Weed). Lennie can't remember important logistical details, but he remembers every single detail about their dream to own a ranch.

In this opening scene, we get snapshots of the two main characters, who are great foils for each other. George is responsible and practical. His main preoccupation, aside from survival, is keeping Lennie under control. We see this in the dead mouse incident—an indication of Lennie's innocent simplicity—which is the first foreshadowing that he doesn't know his own strength and accidentally kills things he only wants to pet and care for.

Point of No Return

James Scott Bell talks about a story having two "doorways of no return." The first doorway pushes the characters into the story, where they're stuck. The second doorway pushes them toward the climax. In *Of Mice and Men*, the first doorway is the new job on the ranch. George and Lennie need this money. Once they arrive, they have no real choice but to stay.

Rising Action

The first person they meet on the ranch is Candy, an important character because of his vulnerability. He's elderly, has only one hand, and has an old dog that's on its last legs. Candy's relationship with the dog mirrors the way people view George's relationship with Lennie. The dog isn't of any use anymore, but it is Candy's companion and he cares for it. The trouble is, Candy isn't of any use anymore either, and he knows it. He has no job security and could be let go at any moment.

The boss's son, Curley, is the antagonist. When he walks into the bunkhouse, he immediately senses weakness in Lennie and picks on him. As Candy tells them later, Curley is the type who picks on big guys because he's small and wishes he was big. Both George and Lennie sense he will be dangerous. Even at this early stage of the novel, Steinbeck is laying the foundation for the tragedy to come. George admits he's scared and makes Lennie repeat what he must do if there's a problem (hide at the riverside where the novella began).

And then in comes Curley's new wife. A good obstacle in a story will amplify the stakes, and Curley's wife doesn't disappoint. If Curley is dangerous, his pretty wife is doubly so. The reader has already suspected this job won't go well; when Lennie can't take his eyes off her, we know for sure. Even before she shows up, we are already prejudiced against her, having heard from Candy that she's "a tart" who flirts with everyone. She is the only female character in the novel, as well as being the only one without a name. She's the archetypal temptress, but there's more to her than the characters (and readers) assume.

As soon as Curley's wife has left the bunkhouse, Lennie shouts that he doesn't like this place and wants to leave. George agrees—but they're stuck here. They have to stay if they want to make enough money to buy their ranch.

Midpoint

The character of Slim provides a contrast to Curley. He treats George and Lennie with dignity and sees the goodness and innocence in Lennie's character. When he mentions that his dog has had pups, two things come of it. Lennie wants one to take care of, and Carlson wants Candy to shoot his old dog (because old = useless) and replace it with one of the pups.

At the midpoint of the novella, Carlson browbeats Candy into letting him shoot the old dog because it smells bad. This mercy killing is another instance of foreshadowing, though Carlson doesn't shoot Candy's dog out of mercy. He shoots it for selfish reasons. Candy realizes he should have been the one to shoot the dog, even though he didn't want to.

Lennie's mishandling of Slim's pups is (yes) more foreshadowing. Lennie has already accidentally killed mice. We know things won't go well with those pups. At the same time, Curley is looking for his wife again—more foreshadowing. There's not a single extraneous detail in this novella.

False Victory

When George and Lennie talk about the ranch they plan to buy, Candy reveals he has money saved up thanks to the compensation he received for the loss of his hand. Candy has seen what happens to a creature that no one has any use for and realizes that going in on the ranch might be his way to achieve security. Suddenly the dream that has been mostly a fantasy becomes a plan with practical steps forward. For the first time, these characters have hope.

Rising Action

When Curley returns to the bunkhouse and misreads Lennie's smile as a taunt, he attacks—and Lennie accidentally crushes Curley's hand. No one blames him for this, however, and Slim warns Curley to tell everyone he got the hand caught in a machine.

The story shifts to Crooks, the only Black character in the novella. How people treat Crooks is an echo of how they treat Lennie—again, a true revelation of character. It's interesting (but not surprising) to see who disregards the racial barriers and who enforces them, who treats Crooks with dignity and who treats him like an animal.

Crooks is forced to live apart from everyone else in the harness room by the manure pile. Steinbeck shows us his humanity immediately, not only by the fastidious way he keeps his room, but also by the books he owns and the pain in his crooked spine. When Lennie visits him (which no one is supposed to do), he is mystified by Crooks' exclusion from the bunkhouse.

Lennie isn't supposed to tell anyone about the ranch plans, but of course it's all he can think about, so he tells Crooks. Crooks recognizes the similarities between them: they are both disregarded, ignored. The difference, however, is that Lennie has George. George is the reason Lennie hasn't been sent to "the booby hatch."

Because Lennie has already crossed the racial barrier and is sitting in Crooks' room, when Candy arrives, he too comes in. Candy reinforces Lennie's talk about the ranch, and Crooks realizes this is a real plan. He offers to come in on the deal and work for nothing. Suddenly, he too has hope.

And then Curley's wife shows up. "They left all the weak ones here," she says—and she's right. The most vulnerable characters are teaming up. When she threatens Crooks with lynching, he transforms from someone who had a glimpse of dignity into a cowering animal. In this way, Steinbeck highlights the dehumanizing effects of both discrimination and segregation.

All Is Lost

Given all the foreshadowing, the novella now hurtles toward a terrible climax that the reader knows is coming. Rather than using the suspense of a surprise event, Steinbeck harnesses the full power of dread as Lennie realizes he has accidentally killed a pup.

This time when Curley's wife appears, Lennie is alone. There is no one to protect him. Lennie knows he isn't supposed to talk to her, and he tries not to, but Curley's wife confesses that she's lonely. She had a dream, rather like the dream of owning a ranch. Hers was to be in the movies. She only married Curley out of spite and now regrets it.

We know this scene will turn bad, and it does. But Steinbeck does something interesting in this moment. By sharing the backstory on

Curley's wife, he has already humanized her, making her into more than just the tart everyone assumes her to be. After Lennie accidentally kills her, we see her essential goodness: "...the meanness and the plannings and the discontent and the ache for attention were all gone from her face," all of which had been created by loneliness and a lack of hope. What Steinbeck seems to be asserting here is that people are essentially good.

Loneliness is another antagonist in this book, and it pops up everywhere. "A guy needs somebody—to be near him," Crooks says. "A guy goes nuts if he ain't got nobody. Don't make no difference who the guy is, long's he's with you...." George plays solitaire. Even the setting's name, Soledad, is the Spanish word for solitude.

Lennie knows he has done something bad. This is the second doorway of no return that pushes the story toward the climax. It's also a plot reversal—the moment when the protagonist's goal must change. Carlson's Luger is missing, and everyone assumes Lennie has stolen it. The men team up to search for Lennie with the intention of lynching him. George attempts to send them in the wrong direction, hoping that Lennie has remembered what to do in case of an emergency (return to the riverside), but he has also stolen the Luger. If worse comes to worst, there's only one other way to protect Lennie now.

The Tragic Climax

Steinbeck returns us to the pristine setting of the opening, with one important difference. The natural world that was so hospitable in the beginning has suddenly become threatening. The animal world is made up of predator and prey. Lennie is alone, and he's being hunted like an animal.

While George is able to kill Lennie with mercy to save him from a worse fate—the very thing Candy could not do with his dog—the fact that he must kill him at all is where the tragedy lies. Yes, George succeeds in his goal of protecting Lennie, but if this is what counts as success, it seems like a rather low bar. The failure is in the circumstances. This world is too harsh for someone like Lennie. It crushes innocence. There is a fundamental lack of compassion, an inability to treat people with dignity. Lennie dies imagining the ranch that he will now never have—and we're pretty sure George will never get it either.

Hope is human. Companionship is human. Caring for the vulnerable is human. But no matter how you look at it, shooting someone in the back of the head like an animal that needs to be put down is not human.

Resolution

George's protective relationship with Lennie echoes all the animals that Lennie tried but failed to take care of and killed instead. George, too, has failed to take care of Lennie and has killed him. However, loneliness does not triumph in the end—there's a suggestion that George and Slim will team up and find friendship. Slim is one of the few characters who understands George and Lennie's friendship as an antidote to loneliness. The book ends with that small glimmer of hope, though companionship is misunderstood by Curley and Carlson right to the last word.

English Teachers Must LOVE This Book

There are endless patterns of imagery and themes to trace:

- The significance of smallness: Lennie Small is big in stature but small in comprehension. George is small, but it doesn't seem to bother him, whereas Curley suffers from "short man syndrome" and feels the need to push his weight around and threaten everyone. There is small-mindedness, smallness as vulnerability, and all the small animals that Lennie kills with love.

- All those hands: They are ranch hands. Candy is missing a hand. Curley wears a glove on one hand filled with Vaseline to keep it soft for his wife. Lennie crushes his other hand, making him vulnerable and more like Candy. Lennie's hands are likened to paws.
- The use of archetypes. Many of the characters in this novella are archetypal:
    - Candy: the sage
    - Curley's wife: the temptress
    - Slim: the leader
    - Lennie: the fool or the innocent
    - George: Everyman
- The use of animal imagery to describe Lennie, leading to the question of what makes us human. What distinguishes us from animals? When we treat people as less than human, what happens to them? What happens to us?

Why Is *Of Mice and Men* a Classic?

Aside from being a brilliant portrayal of what it means to be human, it is Steinbeck's use of the objective POV that makes this novella so important. It doesn't preach or attempt in any way to tell the reader how to think, which is perhaps what makes conservative leaders and small-minded high school teachers so nervous. In an interesting extension of Hemingway's *The Old Man and the Sea*, the POV of this book not only allows space for readers to think for themselves but it demands it. We must decide what we think about Lennie's tragedy. We must decide how we feel about the way Crooks is treated and that Carlson shoots Candy's old dog, how we feel about friendship and hope and dignity. How we feel about Curley's wife. None of this is spoon-fed to us. It simply appears on the page; what we do with it is up to us. This is one reason why it's such a perfect book to teach—it opens discussion on difficult topics like racism and the treatment of people with disabilities.

There have been many conversations about why we read fiction, what it does besides entertain us. Above all else, a good work of fiction teaches not just compassion but also empathy. It forces us into a different pair of shoes, allows us to see the world in a new way, and maybe even gives us the impetus to change it. It does this better than anything else we can think of other than the direct experience of hardship.

Chapter Summary: Of Dreams and Desolation

Of Mice and Men should be required reading for anyone who wants to understand how to create thematic cohesion through the use of symbolism and how to intentionally build a sense of dread. It shows us the power of cohesive imagery and reminds us to trust our reader. Readers are smart. If we give them space to think, they become active participants in the process of reading and are allowed to form their own interpretations of the work.

The Objective Point of View: The objective point of view is a narrative perspective wherein the author presents events and characters without access to their internal thoughts or feelings. Instead, the story unfolds through observable actions, dialogue, and descriptions, compelling readers to infer motivations and emotions based on external cues. In *Of Mice and Men*, Steinbeck employs this technique to great effect. Characters like George and

Lennie are revealed through their interactions and spoken words, allowing readers to engage actively with the narrative by interpreting underlying emotions and themes. This approach enhances the story's realism and invites deeper contemplation of the characters' struggles and the societal issues depicted.

In Medias Res: This is a Latin term meaning "in the middle of things." It refers to a storytelling technique wherein a narrative begins in the midst of action or significant events rather than at the chronological start of the story. This method creates immediate intrigue and urgency as readers piece together prior happenings through dialogue, flashbacks, or gradual revelations. In *Of Mice and Men*, Steinbeck begins the novella after the inciting incident—Lennie's trouble in Weed—has already occurred. As George and Lennie journey to a new ranch job, readers learn about their past and the circumstances that led them there through their conversations. This technique engages readers from the outset and builds suspense as the full context unfolds.

Two Doorways of No Return: In his book *Write Great Fiction: Plot & Structure*, James Scott Bell discusses the two doorways of no return that typically appear in three-act structure—two critical turning points that irrevocably commit the protagonist to the story's central journey and climax. The first doorway thrusts the character into the main conflict, eliminating the option to return to their previous life. The second doorway propels them toward the climax, often escalating the stakes or introducing a significant obstacle. Often, the second doorway will coincide with the all-is-lost moment in the novel. But it can also be an *aha* moment, where the protagonist discovers something important. Either way, it is the door they must step through in order for the climax to be possible.

In *Of Mice and Men*, the first doorway occurs when George and Lennie arrive at the new ranch. Despite sensing potential trouble—especially with characters like Curley and his wife—they have no choice but to stay and work to achieve their dream of owning a ranch. The second doorway happens after Lennie accidentally kills Curley's wife. This irreversible action seals his fate, pushing the narrative inexorably toward the tragic climax.

Part Two: Getting Creative

We now move into the slightly more complex novels in which the authors manipulate three-act structure in more challenging ways. It's worth noting that these decisions are not random; the authors don't make them simply to be fancy. The structure suits the needs of the work.

In writing, any rule can be broken or manipulated... if it's done well. However, you need to know the rules first before you can start breaking them—and you should have a good reason for doing so. As one of our MFA instructors taught us: don't mess with structure unless the work demands it, else it will feel gimmicky and contrived. As you'll see, none of these novels feel that way.

Some of the structural unicorns we'll meet in this section include an apparently missing protagonist, the division of internal and external conflict between two characters, a structure that proceeds in a series of episodes, and the overlay of two trajectories. We've also thrown in a hero's journey structure for good measure that offers the added bonus of a very delayed inciting incident.

Let's dig in!

The Great Gatsby

by F. Scott Fitzgerald

Passive Protagonist Syndrome

We were recently discussing what we refer to as Passive Protagonist Syndrome on social media. This is something developmental editors commonly encounter in manuscripts by new writers. A passive protagonist floats through a story, propelled by the actions and decisions of other characters, rather than providing the plot momentum that is so important to *emotional draw*—the quality of a narrative that keeps readers engaged, anticipatory, and most importantly turning pages.

During this discussion, someone pointed to *The Great Gatsby* by F. Scott Fitzgerald as an example of a successful novel with a (supposedly) passive protagonist, as if that was proof enough that no new writers need concern themselves with active causality. However, there is nothing passive about Fitzgerald's protagonist. While *The Great Gatsby* has at first glance an unusual narrative structure, it does not in fact break any craft fundamentals.

What Does It Mean for a Protagonist to Be Active?

When we talk about *action* or *activity* in terms of narrative structure, we are not necessarily referring to fight scenes or car chases. Instead, activity is about *causality*. A protagonist is active when they make choices and take risks that in some way shape what will happen next. For this reason, a protagonist needs a goal that is clear, specific, and relatable. This goal crystallizes in the inciting incident and is resolved one way or another in the climax. Rising action flows out of the protagonist's efforts toward achieving this goal and creates that nice, neat trajectory from inciting incident to climax that gives a novel cohesion.

Carraway the Detective

Here's where F. Scott Fitzgerald was doing something interesting with the narrative structure of this novel. *The Great Gatsby* is narrated by Nick Carraway, but the protagonist is in fact Jay Gatsby. Carraway is the "view from a single window" that unearths Gatsby's story in both the present and the past.

As the narrator, Carraway is not obliged to provide the plot momentum. That job belongs to Gatsby, the protagonist. However, while there is a passive element to Carraway's window into these events, he is active in his own way—his quest is one of social investigation. He is a detective trying to figure out what the heck is going on with his cousin Daisy Buchanan, which in turn leads him to seek the truth behind Jay Gatsby's past and his efforts to convince Daisy to leave her husband, Tom Buchanan, and marry Gatsby instead.

Carraway's investigation mostly involves hanging out and talking to people or listening, but he actively makes himself available so that he can discover these truths. Since Daisy's former connection to Gatsby is part of the unhappiness in her marriage, the two plot questions become intertwined, especially once she begins her affair with Gatsby. Essentially, Carraway finds himself in the midst of someone else's story, and what his investigation ultimately reveals is the first half of the tragic love affair between Gatsby and Daisy years earlier.

Bit by bit, he unearths the story in reverse: Gatsby's rising action (his efforts in pursuit of wealth, such that he might win Daisy back), Gatsby's inciting incident, and finally Gatsby's stasis and backstory. Indeed, Gatsby's inciting incident and stasis *are* the mystery behind what drove Daisy and Tom apart, much of which is delivered at the end in a final conversation between Nick and Gatsby in a way very similar to the summary of a murder investigation delivered by the sleuth at the end of a detective novel. Classic mystery resolution.

Let's zoom in to examine Gatsby's plot in full.

PLOT POINTS

Stasis

Keep in mind, a story's stasis can include anything leading up to the inciting incident. It is the protagonist's normal life before they set out on their quest. For Gatsby, this includes his youthful desire to be wealthy, to stake his claim on the American Dream. But it also includes his initial romance with Daisy. Young Gatsby and Daisy meet and fall in love when he is a soldier. The potential for marriage and lifelong love constitutes the stakes—that which Gatsby is desperate to hold on to.

(As noted earlier, the stasis, inciting incident, and initial rising action are a mystery for Nick Carraway to uncover. The novel doesn't start until the midpoint.)

Inciting Incident

While Gatsby is deployed overseas, Daisy grows tired of waiting for him to return and marries Tom Buchanan instead. When Gatsby finds out, he is fueled with a desire to win her back. His narrative goal has solidified. He always wanted to be rich—that is integral to his character. But now he has a clear, specific, and relatable reason to become wealthy. Gatsby believes that if he can ascend to Daisy's socioeconomic standing, he will convince her to leave her husband and marry him instead.

Rising Action

Gatsby works hard to succeed in business. He wants to be on comparable economic footing with Daisy's husband, Tom. He achieves this in part through some shady business relationships and by selling bootleg liquor through pharmacies. Eventually, when he has amassed enough of a fortune, he moves to Long Island, across the bay from Daisy, and hosts frequent parties in the hopes that she will one day attend. It is at this point that Gatsby hits a roadblock—he throws party after party, and while he makes the acquaintance of Jordan Baker, Daisy's good friend, his love never shows up at his mansion.

Midpoint

A new opportunity arises for Gatsby when Nick Carraway rents a bungalow next door to Gatsby's mansion. Jordan, whom Nick is dating, informs Gatsby that Nick is Daisy's cousin, and thus Gatsby makes a point of engaging Nick, getting to know him, and eventually arranging a reunion with Daisy at Nick's bungalow.

False Victory

As we've discussed, in a traditional (comic) narrative this would be an all-is-lost moment. However, Gatsby's romantic quest is a tragedy. So it is at this point in the story that he seems closest to victory. He and Daisy have declared their love for each other, and the truth is soon to come out.

Climax and Plot Twist

The affair between Daisy and Gatsby progresses until Tom gets suspicious, and then Gatsby and Tom argue in a Plaza Hotel suite. This is Gatsby's opportunity to pull Daisy away from Tom once and for all. However, Gatsby is overly insistent that Daisy has never loved Tom, which isn't the case, and Tom reveals that Gatsby's wealth has come through shady connections and bootlegging. By the end of the conversation, Daisy's opinion of Gatsby has soured. Tom, now cocksure that his wife will not leave him, asks Gatsby to drive Daisy home so they can talk it over. When they leave, Daisy insists on driving.

Earlier, Tom borrowed Gatsby's distinctive yellow car, so when Gatsby and Daisy are on their way back from the Plaza Hotel, Myrtle Wilson, Tom's mistress, sees the car and runs out to flag Tom down. They have all been drinking, and so Daisy loses control, hitting Myrtle and killing her, then flees. Gatsby accepts the blame. Later, when Tom visits the scene and talks to Myrtle's husband, George, he reveals that Gatsby owns the car, thereby implying that Gatsby was Myrtle's lover *and* the cause of her death. This drives George into a rage in which he murders Gatsby and then kills himself.

Resolution

In the climax, once Nick learns that Daisy was the one driving and that Gatsby was taking the fall for her, he finally comes around to fully empathizing with the self-made millionaire. After the murder-suicide, he dedicates himself to getting in touch with anyone who might attend Gatsby's funeral. Eventually he meets Gatsby's father and thus fills in the final pieces of the Great Jay Gatsby's backstory.

Why Is *The Great Gatsby* a Classic?

Is *The Great Gatsby* an example of a novel with a passive protagonist? No, certainly not. Gatsby perfectly fits the bill of an active protagonist who drives the momentum of his own story from beginning to tragic end. The novel explores universal themes: the American Dream, the decline of morality, the destructive nature of greed, and the elusive nature of happiness. All of these themes resonate with readers in any era.

Chapter Summary: A Protagonist in Disguise

Keep in mind that story structure is more about convincing readers to keep turning pages than it is about how to write a novel. Within the dimensions of narrative structure, there are limitless possibilities. To repeat a metaphor from the introduction: think of narrative structure as a painter's canvas. Even though the edges of the canvas are defined, an author still has full creative potential when it comes to what happens within that framework. Structure—how we play with it, how we use it to tell a story—is an integral part of the art form.

But you have to know the rules before you decide to break them. Fitzgerald's decisions are the result of careful manipulation rather than sloppy judgment. He uses structure to create mystery, thereby also increasing emotional draw. Through Nick Carraway, we enter Gatsby's story at the midpoint. The protagonist's stasis, inciting incident, and half of his rising action all happen "off-screen" and are therefore revealed as backstory. But the foundational plot elements are there, even if they appear in an unconventional arrangement.

Passive Protagonist: A passive protagonist is a main character who does not actively influence the plot through their decisions or actions. Instead, they are carried along by events initiated by others. This can lead to a narrative in which the protagonist lacks agency, making it challenging for readers to engage with their journey. In contrast, an active protagonist drives the story forward with clear goals and decisive actions. In *The Great Gatsby*, Jay Gatsby is not a passive protagonist. He actively orchestrates his reunion with Daisy Buchanan by acquiring wealth, hosting extravagant parties to attract her attention, and involving Nick Carraway in his plans—all of which propel the plot.

Causal Trajectory: An active protagonist is a character whose deliberate choices and actions create a chain of cause and effect that moves the narrative forward. This causal trajectory follows a logical sequence where one event leads to another: an action occurs, causing a consequence, which prompts another action, and so on. Plot causality is essential for building momentum and maintaining reader interest. An active protagonist's pursuit of their goals generates conflict, tension, and progression—and it also demonstrates who they are, what matters to them, and what they are willing to do (or not) to get what they want. Thus, causality is also integral to strong characterization.

Narrator Versus Protagonist: The narrator is the voice or character who tells the story to the reader, as per their distinct perspective and analysis. The protagonist is the central character whose actions and decisions are the primary focus and driver of the story's plot. While the narrator and protagonist are often the same person, they can be distinct. Note that we saw this in Melville's *Moby-Dick*, in which Ishmael is the narrator while Ahab is the protagonist—and we will also see it in *Wuthering Heights*. In *The Great Gatsby*, Nick Carraway serves as the narrator, offering his observations and interpretations of the events and characters. Jay Gatsby, on the other hand, is the protagonist whose pursuit of Daisy Buchanan drives the plot. Nick's role as an observer and confidant allows readers to explore Gatsby's world through an external lens: the "view from a single window."

The Scarlet Letter

by Nathaniel Hawthorne

Hester's Ordeal and Dimmesdale's Agony

In our work as developmental editors, we frequently encounter protagonists who do not have a fleshed-out internal conflict. The external conflict is clear, but without an internal conflict running interference, it can be difficult for readers to connect with the protagonist. But in *The Scarlet Letter*, Nathaniel Hawthorne takes a different approach. There is indeed an entanglement of external and internal conflict, but he hands each of these to two different characters.

The Scarlet Letter is a historical fiction novel (published in 1850 but set in the 1640s) about a young couple whose tryst goes badly when a pregnancy reveals their affair. Hester Prynne was married in England and sent on to Boston by her husband, Roger Chillingworth, who was supposed to follow soon after. When he doesn't arrive and she gives him up for dead, she falls for the local preacher, Arthur Dimmesdale, and gets pregnant. Since the community knows Hester to be married, she is condemned as an adulteress and forced to wear a scarlet letter *A* in public to brand her. Her lover, meanwhile, remains unidentified.

Narrative Goals

We have two protagonists on our hands. We also have an active antagonist in Roger Chillingworth, with a plotline of his own. Let's consider the story from all three perspectives:

- When Hester Prynne is forced to wear the scarlet letter for adultery, she must navigate societal rejection and seek personal redemption to rebuild her life and protect her daughter, lest isolation and stigma destroy both her spirit and her future.

- When Arthur Dimmesdale, a respected minister, conceals his part in Hester Prynne's adultery, he must grapple with his crippling guilt and seek forgiveness, otherwise his unresolved torment threatens to unravel his health and his position in the community.

- When Roger Chillingworth discovers that his wife, Hester Prynne, has borne a child from an adulterous affair while he was presumed lost at sea, he seeks revenge against the child's father. He must plot and execute this revenge without revealing his identity or aspirations for vengeance to the townsfolk.

A Quick Word About the Wacky First Chapter

The Scarlet Letter begins with "The Customs House," a peculiar chapter that serves to establish the narrator and the historical context of the story. In Hawthorne's time, historical fiction as a genre was not well-defined. This chapter sets up the narrator's authority and scope, explaining how he has access to the entire tale and can follow different characters with a classic form of distanced, commentary-heavy omniscience.

This narrative choice allows Hawthorne to explore the internal and external conflicts of multiple characters. However, his approach also creates significant distance between the reader and the characters. Modern readers, editors, and publishers often expect the story to dive directly into the plot. We've also come to prefer more intimate narration, such as a deep third-person POV, which connects us more directly to the characters' experiences.

Despite these shifts in narrative preferences, Hawthorne's choice of a distanced omniscient narrator serves his story well. It provides a grand, sweeping view of Puritan society and its complexities. While this style may not be in vogue today, it effectively sets the stage for the intertwined lives and conflicts of Hester, Dimmesdale, and Chillingworth.

That being said, some readers will understandably skip this long-winded and summary-heavy first chapter and dive right into Hester's tale.

An Externalized Internal Conflict

In real life, people have many internal conflicts, which means that a protagonist should too. Everything bouncing around inside a character's head contributes to their complexity and, therefore, their authenticity. But when we talk about internal conflict in fiction, we're not just referring to a distant worry or a momentary spike in anxiety. In order to create and sustain emotional draw (that quality of a narrative that keeps readers anticipatory and thus turning pages), authors stack obstacles in front of their protagonist. The internal conflict is often the biggest obstacle of all. It is something the protagonist must come to terms with before their narrative goal can be achieved.

In *The Scarlet Letter*, Hester Prynne has many legitimate worries. The townsfolk question whether she should be allowed to keep her daughter. She also wants to be redeemed in the eyes of God. But these concerns are directly related to her external conflict—her narrative goal—which is to overcome public shame. She doesn't have a clear misbelief or fatal flaw that she needs to come to terms with. A fatal flaw will indeed become her biggest obstacle. But the flaw doesn't belong to her; it belongs to Arthur Dimmesdale.

As a respected young minister in the seventeenth-century Puritan community of Boston, Dimmesdale has a lot to lose. So when Hester becomes pregnant, the couple decides to keep his name out of it. This leads to intense guilt and self-loathing on Dimmesdale's part, which manifests in his failing health. While Hester has a lot stacked against her, it is Dimmesdale's guilt that brings her closest to failure. And while Hester is active in the pursuit of her narrative goal, Dimmesdale is not. To put that another way, Hester is internally passive while Dimmesdale is externally passive. Their external and internal activity combine to create a complete arc that neither would have on their own.

Nathaniel Hawthorne splits the arc between these two characters for thematic reasons. Hester and Dimmesdale are two parts of a whole: public shame versus private shame, sin versus redemption, courage versus cowardice. An important takeaway here is that when an author breaks a "rule" or craft fundamental, it works best when done intentionally. After all, craft fundamentals are about taking the reader's experience into account. If you're going to rock the structural boat, you should have a reason for doing so, and that reason should serve the story.

Even though Hester and Dimmesdale are two parts of a whole, not all their plot points line up. Let's take a look.

PLOT POINTS—Hester Prynne

Stasis

The story opens in rising action—after the inciting incident, and even after the point of no return, so Hester's stasis is only hinted at. She arrives in Boston ahead of her husband, an older man whom she doesn't love, and after time passes and she assumes he has died, Hester enters into an affair with Dimmesdale.

Structurally, a story's stasis is important because it provides the foundation for the protagonist's motivation, and it is out of this motivation that the narrative goal forms. To put that another way, a stasis motivation is a generalized desire or value that tells us something about the protagonist's underlying character, while the narrative goal is specific—it is the source of plot.

Hester's motivation is to live righteously, which is manifested in her daughter Pearl. Her narrative goal is to overcome public shame, a necessity not only for herself but also for Pearl. If Hester cannot regain some respect in the community, she risks losing her daughter.

Inciting Incident

The moment Hester's narrative goal comes together is when she receives her sentence. For the rest of her days, she must wear a scarlet letter *A* upon her chest as a proclamation of her sin. With that stigma as a constant reminder for all to see, she must find a way to overcome her public shame.

Point of No Return

In a phenomenal statement about her character, Hester embroiders her scarlet letter with exceptional skill, even fashioning it with gold thread. She does so in defiance of Puritan austerity, which in itself is a risk, but it is also a statement about her worth to the community—that she is an excellent seamstress. She could flee Boston and start a new life elsewhere, but instead she commits to staying, and this starts with an advertisement of her skills. This is her opportunity to secure the work that she will need to provide for her daughter. She will live her sin publicly while also claiming a place in the community.

Rising Action

Here is where the story begins: Hester is released from prison with Pearl in her arms and the scarlet letter on her chest. She is forced to stand on a scaffold in front of the gathered townsfolk, and in a negative coincidence, her not-so-dead husband appears at the back of the crowd.

(This opening scene serves as the antagonist's inciting incident: her husband, Roger Chillingworth, decides to keep his identity a secret from the community so that he can root out Hester's baby-daddy—more on that in a minute.)

Keeping in mind that Hester's narrative goal is to overcome her public shame, her rising action involves how she struggles and strives toward this end, much of which involves her daughter. Pearl is a bit wild, such that her mother wonders if she's fully human. The girl's tendency for tantrums and defiance threatens to undermine Hester's efforts at redeeming herself in the eyes of the community. However, Hester lives her sin out in the open, and instead of suppressing or denying Pearl's wild nature, she dresses her daughter in ornate clothing—scarlet and gold to match the letter upon her chest—highlighting her daughter as both a symbol of her transgression and her own refusal to conceal the consequences of her actions.

This conflict comes to a head early on when Governor Bellingham suggests that Hester isn't fit to raise the child. She implores

Reverend Dimmesdale to vouch for her, which he does, and this resolves the threat to her custody of Pearl.

More and more, the townsfolk turn to Hester to make and mend their clothing. After a while, even the town's magistrates wear her garments. But as Hester becomes more accepted, as her scarlet letter comes to stand for "able" and perhaps "acceptance," she herself becomes more severe and dresses more plainly, like the rest of the Puritan townsfolk. Such is the pious humility she has gained—her public badge of sin is the source of her redemption.

As such, Hester's stakes are somewhat resolved early on, at least in terms of the direct threat to her custody of Pearl. However, trouble is on the horizon with Chillingworth and Dimmesdale.

Midpoint Reversal

All this time, Chillingworth has been tormenting Dimmesdale while also acting as the ailing man's doctor. When Hester realizes what her husband is up to, she confronts him, admonishes him for what he is doing to the reverend, and threatens to reveal his true identity. This point in the novel is a reversal since the protagonist's goal shifts. She has come a long way toward overcoming her public shame and gaining the community's acceptance. Now that she is at her strongest and Dimmesdale is at his weakest, she wants to help him. This is also a reversal of the opening scenario, when she was at her weakest and he was at his strongest. Thus, her new goal is to help Dimmesdale overcome his demons—or rather, his singular demon: Chillingworth.

Rising Action

Hester follows Dimmesdale as he sets out to visit a Native American village. When she finds him in the forest, she confesses that Chillingworth is her husband and insists that they leave Boston together. Up to this point, it has been Hester's love of Pearl that has driven her onward. Now she makes a gambit for Dimmesdale's love. But she does so out of a desire to help him—to do for him what he couldn't do for her. Dimmesdale agrees to the plan. They will sail back to England together.

However, when Hester tosses aside her scarlet letter, Pearl becomes upset. Though young, Pearl has grown up with the letter as a constant presence, one she instinctively understands as central to her mother's identity. When Dimmesdale gives Pearl a kiss, she washes it off in the brook. Though she may not fully understand the intricacies of her father's guilt, her instinctive rejection reflects her keen perception of authenticity. Dimmesdale's failure to publicly acknowledge her or Hester undermines the love he offers in private.

All Is Lost—the Dark Moment

The plan is for Dimmesdale to deliver his Election Day sermon, after which he, Hester, and Pearl will secretly board a ship to England. However, since the meeting in the forest, Dimmesdale's inner turmoil has only deepened. Meanwhile, Hester learns that Chillingworth has booked passage on the same ship. If their planned departure is discovered before they leave, they risk both public disgrace and potential legal repercussions. Hester could face renewed punishment for her perceived transgressions, and Dimmesdale might be charged with adultery—destroying not only his reputation but also their chance of starting anew as a family. The shadow of Puritan law looms over their plans, compounding the stakes of their escape.

Climax

Hester has done everything she can. The next move is up to Dimmesdale—it is finally the passive co-protagonist's turn to act. The reverend delivers the best sermon of his life, eliciting cheers and shouts from the congregation, and he knows it is also his last. His health is failing him, and he cannot go on with the lie he has held for so long. Running away was never really an option, because that would only compound his sin. Reverend Dimmesdale calls Hester and Pearl to join him on the village scaffold, and then he makes his shocking confession. It's now Pearl's turn to kiss her father—he has atoned, so she can finally forgive him. Dimmesdale promises Hester that they will be together again in heaven, and then he drops dead, right there on the scaffold, from the illness that has been eating at him.

Resolution

Hester and Pearl remain in Boston, and within the year, Chillingworth dies, leaving all his wealth to Pearl. Mother and daughter return to England for a time, but eventually Hester sails back to Boston. She puts the scarlet letter back on and dedicates her life to helping others. When she dies, she is buried next to Dimmesdale beneath a single headstone engraved with nothing but the letter *A*.

PLOT POINTS—Arthur Dimmesdale

Stasis

Hawthorne doesn't come right out and say that Dimmesdale is Hester's lover and Chillingworth is her husband, even though it becomes obvious fairly quickly. But as a result, the narrator doesn't reveal any specifics about Dimmesdale's stasis—apart from the fact that he's a reverend, so clearly the state of his soul and his reputation are both very important to him.

Inciting Incident

As with Hester, Dimmesdale's inciting incident is the pregnancy scandal. The townsfolk know Hester is married, even if it is to a man they've never met. While Hester cannot hide her involvement, Dimmesdale can. Since the story begins after this point, readers don't learn exactly how the two lovers agreed to keep this secret, but a secret it is, nonetheless. In the opening scene, it's clear the baby's father hasn't come forward, and when pressed, Hester refuses to name him. Dimmesdale's narrative goal is set: he must keep this secret while wrestling with the guilt of both his sin and his cowardice.

Note the difference in specificity of these two narrative goals. Hester's goal has a potential finish line: she may well reach a point when the community as a whole accepts her and the threat to her custody of Pearl has ended—and in fact, she largely achieves her goal by the midpoint, necessitating a reversal. However, Dimmesdale's goal, *to contend with guilt*, does not have a finish line. If he keeps his secret, his guilt will remain. This is quite common in tragic structure. The fatal flaw drives the protagonist to pursue a goal they cannot hope to achieve (and probably shouldn't want to). In a comic structure, as we see with Hester, the reader cheers the protagonist on toward their goal. In a tragic structure, the reader cheers the protagonist to give up on their misguided goal and instead do the right thing.

Point of No Return

Shortly after the story begins, both a church leader and the governor urge a reluctant Reverend Dimmesdale to get Hester's confession. Here is his opportunity, with the entire town present, to own up to the affair. Instead, he continues the farce and weakly asks Hester to name her lover. She refuses. Their lie has been performed in front of everyone. Now more than ever, Dimmesdale is stuck. He must carry this lie and the guilt that comes with it.

Rising Action

Whereas Hester's rising action centers around Pearl, Dimmesdale's rising action is tied to Chillingworth. When the governor suggests taking Pearl away from Hester, Dimmesdale insists that the child remain with her. Chillingworth is present for this, so it is his first major clue as to who Hester might have had an affair with. From the reader's perspective, it seems like the gig might be up, but in fact Chillingworth doesn't want to expose Dimmesdale; he wants to torment him.

And torment him he does. Dimmesdale knows Chillingworth is watching him, but there's nothing he can do about it. His health is worsening, and the doctor, who spent time studying medicine in Native American communities prior to his arrival in Boston, has a remedy to keep the reverend going. It's not a cure though; it seems the doctor has no intention of curing him.

The more Dimmesdale's health declines, the more the townsfolk think he's a saint. Their admiration only increases his guilt.

Midpoint

The midpoint of Dimmesdale's plotline is the midpoint for the entire novel. He goes to the scaffold one night, more tortured than ever, when Hester and Pearl happen upon him. They mount the steps and hold hands with him. Pearl asks Dimmesdale if he will join them on the scaffold the following afternoon—she senses the lie between them, hidden as they are by the night. After a shooting star appears as a letter *A* above them, Chillingworth shows up and leads Dimmesdale away. The reverend is no doubt afraid that his secret has finally been revealed, and Chillingworth is more certain than ever of Dimmesdale's sin.

Note that this is a midpoint but not a reversal for Arthur. As a midpoint, it finally gives readers insight into Hester and Dimmesdale's affair, and it increases the stakes as Chillingworth is a witness to the reveal. However, Dimmesdale's narrative goal hasn't changed.

False Victory

As we've seen in earlier chapters, the tragic climax is preceded by a false victory rather than an all-is-lost moment. This is the scene in which Hester intercepts Dimmesdale in the woods. He is buoyed by her strength, and her offer for them to run away together fills him with new hope. He does not have to live with this guilt forever. They can leave Boston behind and become the family they always wanted to be.

Tragic Climax

This reprieve proves false when Dimmesdale returns to town. Evil thoughts are creeping into his head. He refuses Chillingworth's medicine, burns his Election Day sermon, and starts writing a new one. He is forced to abandon his misbelief that he can endure this guilt. At last, he is ready to give up on his futile quest.

When it comes time to deliver his inspired sermon, Dimmesdale calls Hester and Pearl up to the scaffold, confesses, and then dies. He has failed at his quest to keep this secret while contending with his guilt. Instead, he makes his public confession and earns the forgiveness of Hester and Pearl. At the same time, he has thwarted Chillingworth's attempt to fully corrupt and damn his soul.

PLOT POINTS—Roger Chillingworth

Stasis

Chillingworth is the most enigmatic of the three main characters. We learn that he delayed his arrival in Boston to spend time with Native Americans, with whom he studied medicine. We also know that he is older than Hester and that she does not love him.

Inciting Incident

Roger Chillingworth arrives to the crowd assembled around the scaffold, where Hester stands, newly released from prison, with baby Pearl in her arms. He knows at once that his wife has had an affair. In this moment, his plan for revenge solidifies, though readers learn this obliquely. Initially, his goal is to find out who the baby's father is, but the undercurrent is already about revenge.

In this scene, all he does is motion for Hester to ignore him. This subtle gesture makes it clear that Chillingworth does not intend to declare himself as Hester's husband. He has other plans, which readers can only guess at.

Point of No Return

When Chillingworth motions to Hester, he takes a step forward in his revenge quest. However, the townspeople still haven't really noticed him. But when baby Pearl begins screaming and Hester panics, Chillingworth introduces himself as a doctor and administers medicine to both mother and daughter. At this point he is stuck in his quest because he has essentially lied to all the townsfolk in not admitting that he is Hester's husband. (And in this scene, he doubles down by making Hester swear not to reveal him.) This will enable him to discover the identity of Pearl's father.

Rising Action

At first, Chillingworth inserts himself into the community so he can wait and watch. His first clue arises when Governor Bellingham suggests taking Pearl from Hester. She appeals to Reverend Dimmesdale, who wholeheartedly vouches for her.

Now that he has his suspect, Chillingworth finds an excuse to get closer to Dimmesdale. The reverend's health is already declining, so the doctor has the perfect reason to move in with him.

Midpoint

One day, Chillingworth catches Dimmesdale watching out the window as Hester and Pearl pass by the house. The reverend's reaction to them is a pretty clear confirmation of the relationship, but just to make sure, Chillingworth rips open Dimmesdale's shirt when he is sleeping, then dances maniacally around the room at whatever he has seen on the reverend's chest. The implication is that Dimmesdale bears a hidden version of the scarlet letter on his chest, and that Chillingworth's vengeance is turning the doctor into an actual devil.

Now that Chillingworth has confirmation that Dimmesdale is Pearl's father, his quest shifts from finding the hidden adulterer to exacting his revenge.

Rising Action

Roger Chillingworth follows the poor Reverend Dimmesdale everywhere. His revenge quest corrupts him to such an extent that the townsfolk see his devilish nature. Indeed, he has become intent on damning Dimmesdale's soul.

False Victory

Chillingworth won't get what he wants in the end, which makes this a tragic structure. Accordingly, the very unchill doctor gets a false victory when he finds out Hester and Dimmesdale's plan to escape to England. When he books passage on the same ship, he has them trapped. Even if they manage to escape Boston, Chillingworth's presence threatens to unravel their plans for a new life, as he will remain a relentless reminder of both their sin and the judgment that follows them.

Tragic Climax

Following the fateful Election Day sermon, when Dimmesdale calls on Hester and Pearl to join him on the scaffold, Chillingworth tries to stop them. But then Dimmesdale makes his confession, ripping open his shirt to reveal the "red stigma" on his chest. And then, properly confessed before the townsfolk—and more importantly, before God—Dimmesdale dies. He has atoned, and therefore he can await Hester in heaven. In other words, the devil in their midst has lost. Chillingworth admits defeat: "Thou hast escaped me!"

Want Versus Need

Some craft guides discuss internal and external conflict as a *want* versus a *need*. The want is the external conflict—the protagonist's efforts toward a narrative goal and all the obstacles that pop up in their path. The need is the internal conflict—something the protagonist must come to terms with before they can achieve their want, or something the protagonist must realize is more important than their want.

As noted earlier, these two elements are split between Hester and Dimmesdale. Hester has the want: to overcome public shame by raising a God-fearing daughter and establishing herself as a reliable and respectable member of the community. Dimmesdale has the need: to overcome his guilt and cowardice. What's interesting is that Dimmesdale's public confession is also what Hester needs. Once the townsfolk realize that their proclaimed saint is the adulterer, they must reconsider their judgment of Hester and Pearl.

Why Is *The Scarlet Letter* a Classic?

Nathaniel Hawthorne's *The Scarlet Letter* endures as a classic largely through its masterful symbolism, which is woven into each sentence. Every aside, every description, carries thematic weight.

For example, each character's name is a key to understanding their symbolic and narrative roles. Governor Bellingham, whose name means "den of bears," mirrors his function as a keeper of societal law and order. Dimmesdale's name reflects his diminishing health and spirit, and the prison that is his sin and guilt. Chillingworth's name conveys the doctor's cold pursuit of vengeance and also his hidden wealth. Pearl represents the beauty that can arise from strife. And Hester Prynne, whose name mean "star," transforms from a symbol of shame into a beacon of strength and altruism—she becomes the saint the townsfolk thought Dimmesdale was.

The Scarlet Letter was a hit when it was first published, and it persists as a classic today because of its intentionality. Every element works double-time in service of the whole, making it a great narrative for writers to study. While the extremely distanced omniscient narrator is a harder sell these days, Hawthorne's underlying strategies for building tension and enriching character arcs with nonstop symbolism offer invaluable insights for modern writers aiming to enhance their own storytelling craft.

Chapter Summary: A Tale of Two Sinners

Nathaniel Hawthorne's *The Scarlet Letter* splits the traditional protagonist role between Hester Prynne and Reverend Arthur Dimmesdale in a unique entanglement of external and internal conflicts. Hester embodies the external struggle against societal condemnation after bearing a child out of wedlock, while Dimmesdale grapples internally with guilt and self-loathing over his concealed sin. Hawthorne's use of a distanced omniscient narrator—established through the peculiar opening chapter, "The Custom House"—allows for a comprehensive exploration of these intertwined lives within the rigid framework of Puritan society.

Internal Versus External: External conflict refers to the struggles a character faces with outside forces, such as other characters, societal norms, or natural obstacles. Internal conflict, on the other hand, occurs within a character's mind, involving emotional turmoil, moral dilemmas, or psychological barriers. These conflicts are often entangled in narrative structure, as the external pressures can exacerbate internal struggles, and internal conflicts can influence how a character responds to external challenges.

Want Versus Need: The want-versus-need paradigm provides another way to think about internal and external conflict—the difference between a character's external desires and their deeper internal requirements for fulfillment. The *want* is the character's conscious goal—what they believe will bring happiness or resolve their problems. The *need* represents an internal deficiency or lesson they must learn to achieve true satisfaction or personal growth.

Misbelief: In her book *Story Genius,* Lisa Cron introduces the concept of a misbelief—a fundamental, mistaken belief that a protagonist holds about themselves or the world, formed from past experiences. This misbelief drives the internal conflict and influences every decision the character makes. According to Cron, for a story to resonate, the protagonist must confront and overcome this misbelief to achieve true growth and attain their external goal.

Applying this to *The Scarlet Letter*, Reverend Dimmesdale's misbelief is that he can atone for his sin privately while maintaining his esteemed position in the community. He believes that public confession would destroy his ability to do good. This fallacy traps him in a cycle of guilt and hypocrisy, which in turn impacts his health. It's only when he confronts and relinquishes this misbelief—by publicly confessing—that he achieves a measure of peace, albeit at the cost of his life.

The Call of the Wild

by Jack London

Buck the Beefcake

We picked up *The Call of the Wild* expecting to revisit a childhood adventure tale. After all, the protagonist is a dog. But diving back in, we were surprised to discover this is no gentle story for kids.

From the first chapter, Buck gets beaten to within an inch of his life. The brutality is stark and unflinching. The writing isn't simplified either. Jack London's prose is complex, rich, and poetic. It's a far cry from the toned-down language typical in today's young adult (YA) and middle grade (MG) books.

Not that young readers can't handle literary prose. *Anne of Green Gables* doesn't shy away from complexity, and children still adore it. But modern standards often favor simpler language and straightforward sentences.

Interestingly, this novel was first published in the *Saturday Evening Post*, a pulp market magazine. It's fair to assume London didn't intend it for children. His audience was adult readers craving adventure and depth.

Another reason this book seems an odd choice for children today is the blatant racism, which we'll discuss later. But what caught us most off guard was how the book at times reads like softcore erotica. London's descriptions of Buck's rippling muscles and raw power made us laugh out loud. More than once, we felt like we were reading a furry parody of an alpha-male romance. The emphasis on Buck's physicality is at times intense, to the point of being cartoonish. It's as if London sought to elevate this dog into a symbol of raw, untamed masculinity.

Narrative Goal

The Call of the Wild traces Buck's transformation from pampered pet to wild creature. Structurally, it's a bildungsroman—a type of coming-of-age story in which the protagonist is in the process of *becoming*. This journey unfolds in four episodes. It's quite common for bildungsroman narratives to be episodic because that kind of structure allows an author to explore various stages of the protagonist's development, highlighting significant events and experiences that shape the main character.

In the first episode, Buck learns to survive in a brutal new world. In the second, he engages in a rivalry with the lead dog. In the third, his leadership is tested under the rule of new masters. And in the final episode, Buck answers the call of the wild.

Let's take a look at how each episode is structured.

PLOT POINTS

Initial Stasis and Catalyst

Before the action of the story begins, Buck, a St. Bernard–Scotch collie mix, lives an easy life on Judge Miller's estate in California. He's treated like royalty, with no exposure to hardship or danger. This stasis serves to establish Buck's identity as a domesticated dog with no concept of survival in the wild. His world is shattered, however, when Manuel, one of the gardener's helpers, kidnaps him to pay off his gambling debts. Buck is eventually sold to Red Sweater Man, who teaches him the "law of club"—a brutal introduction to submission by force. The catalyst sets Buck on the path of transformation from domesticated pet to a creature shaped by the wilderness—one who can survive without humanity's luxuries.

Episode One: Learning the Ropes

Inciting Incident

The first key turning point comes soon after Buck arrives in the Yukon when Curly, a friendly Newfoundland, is attacked and killed by a pack of huskies. Here is Buck's first hard lesson in the "law of fang"—in this new world, one false step can mean death. His initial goal takes shape: he must overcome his soft, sheltered self and learn the ropes of survival.

Rising Action

The narrative now focuses on Buck's struggle to adapt. He observes Spitz, the lead dog, who shows no remorse for Curly's death, foreshadowing their coming rivalry. Buck is soon harnessed and begins learning the brutal and exhausting work of pulling the sled. He watches the experienced sled dogs, especially Dave and Solleks, who teach him to respect the dynamics of the team and the harsh realities of the wild.

Midpoint

On his first night in the wilderness, Buck seeks warmth by trying to enter the humans' tent but is kicked out. Unsure where the other dogs have gone, Buck panics until he discovers that they've burrowed into the snow. This realization—that he must adapt or perish—marks a turning point in his ability to survive. He imitates the other dogs, and in doing so takes another step toward transformation.

Rising Action Continues

As Buck grows more attuned to his new environment, he learns to steal food, copying the sneaky dog Pike. His instincts sharpen, and his muscles harden from the constant work, a sign that he's beginning to master his role in the pack.

Climax

Instead of a dramatic confrontation, this episode closes with a quiet realization: Buck has internalized the lessons of the sled-dog world. He has adapted to the law of club and fang and settled into his new role within the team. His strength and cunning have increased, but the next challenge—the growing rivalry with Spitz—looms.

Episode Two: The Rivalry

Inciting Incident

With Buck now established as a capable sled dog, a new conflict emerges. Spitz, sensing Buck's rising strength, sees him as a threat. This rivalry becomes the new narrative goal: Buck must challenge Spitz's abusive authority and ultimately prove himself worthy of leadership.

Rising Action

Tension builds as Buck and Spitz engage in several conflicts. During a wild husky attack, while the rest of the pack unites against the threat, Spitz tries to ambush Buck. It's also around this time that Buck feels the first stirrings of ancient instincts, in a foreshadowing of the final episode, when the call of the wild finally grips him.

Midpoint

A crucial turning point occurs when Dolly, one of the sled dogs, goes mad with rabies and chases Buck. Exhausted from the chase, Buck is immediately attacked by Spitz, which solidifies Buck's resolve to overthrow his rival. After this incident, Buck challenges Spitz's authority, even preventing him from disciplining the other dogs.

All Is Lost

As the team reaches Dawson, they get a brief respite. The rivalry between Buck and Spitz seems to settle, but this is merely the calm before the storm. The pack is united in their howling at night, but the tension remains beneath the surface. The final push comes during a rabbit chase. Buck and Spitz race to catch a rabbit, but the faster Spitz beats Buck to the prize. However, this moment of defeat is short-lived; it triggers Buck to confront Spitz head-on.

Climax

The climax of this episode is a fierce fight between Buck and Spitz. Though Spitz is more experienced, Buck uses his intelligence to outmaneuver him, eventually breaking Spitz's leg. Buck leaves his injured rival for the other dogs to finish off, cementing his victory.

Resolution

Buck's triumph over Spitz marks his ascent to leadership. His goal has shifted from survival to dominance, and he now takes on the responsibility of leading the pack. His instincts, sharpened through this struggle, prepare him for the next stage of his evolution.

Episode Three: The Challenges of Leadership

Inciting Incident

After defeating Spitz, Buck expects to take the lead position in the team. François initially tries to give the role to Sol-leks, but Buck retaliates, refusing any subordinate position. His goal is now clear: to prove his worth as the pack leader, both to François and his team.

Rising Action

Buck rises to the challenge, showing himself to be a more effective leader than Spitz. Even lazy dogs like Pike work harder under Buck's command, and the team makes record time. However, soon after, François and Perrault are reassigned, and a "Scotch Half-Breed" takes over the team. The workload increases, but Buck continues to lead his disciplined team onward.

Midpoint

The team arrives at Skaguay and is sold to three incompetent owners: Hal, Charles, and Mercedes. This marks a shift, as Buck's leadership skills will now be tested by the poor decision-making of the humans in charge.

Rising Action Continues

The sled is overloaded, and the new owners mishandle the dogs, leading to starvation and exhaustion. Buck's leadership can only do so much under these circumstances, and he loses faith in human authority.

All Is Lost

Buck's strength is nearly depleted. One by one, the dogs are dropping dead. With the pack dwindling, and with Hal, Charles, and Mercedes fighting over trivial matters, Buck is pushed to the brink.

Climax

The turning point comes when they arrive at John Thornton's camp. Thornton warns the incompetent trio that the ice ahead is too thin, but they won't listen. Buck senses the danger and refuses to pull the sled, despite being beaten by Hal. Buck's act of defiance marks the climax of his leadership—he would rather sacrifice himself than lead his team to certain death.

Resolution

John Thornton intervenes and cuts Buck free from the team. Hal, Charles, and Mercedes continue without him, and of course they meet their end when they fall through the ice.

Episode Four: The Call of the Wild

Stasis

Buck enjoys a peaceful life with John Thornton, who treats him with kindness and respect. For the first time, Buck is overcome with love and loyalty for a human. Even back on Judge Miller's farm, he never felt such devotion. However, now that survival is no longer a constant concern, his deeper instincts rise to the surface.

Inciting Incident

The true call of the wild emerges as Buck hears mysterious sounds in the forest which stir something ancient within him. He feels increasingly compelled to explore the wilderness. His final narrative goal is to heed the call of the wild; the remaining obstacle is his devotion to Thornton.

This dilemma presents an impossible choice. Buck's desire to leave humanity behind and seek out a life in the forest is powerful, but so is his loyalty to this man.

Rising Action

Buck proves his loyalty to Thornton through a series of dramatic events, such as saving him from drowning and winning a bet (that Thornton should never have made) by pulling a sled loaded with a thousand pounds. But as his devotion to Thornton increases, so does the lure of the wilderness.

Midpoint

On one of Buck's forays into the forest, he meets a timber wolf. Though they struggle to communicate, there is an undeniable kinship between them as they bound through the woods together. This encounter with the wolf marks the midpoint of this episode. Buck feels torn between his love for Thornton and his growing desire to join the wild. The tension between these two worlds is more pronounced than ever.

Rising Action Continues

Buck spends more and more time away from Thornton, hunting and living as a wild creature. He fully embraces his ancestral beefcake instincts by implausibly tracking and killing a bull moose. Despite this growing independence, his bond with Thornton still holds him back from fully submitting to the wild.

All Is Lost

Buck returns to camp one day to find that John Thornton and his companions have been killed by a group of Yeehat Native

Americans. With the death of the only human he truly loved, Buck loses the last connection to his domesticated life.

Climax

In a scene of unfortunate racism, Buck flies into a rage and attacks the Yeehats, who apparently aren't skilled enough with bow and arrow to take down a single dog. He massacres them in retaliation for Thornton's death. This moment of violence represents Buck's final break from the human world.

Resolution

With nothing left to tie him to human life, Buck answers the call of the wild completely. He joins the wolf pack and becomes a legend among the Yeehats, known as the "Ghost Dog." Buck finds a mate and leads the pack, his offspring carrying both wolf and dog traits—a symbol of Buck's full transformation into a creature of the wild.

Racism and Machismo

Another reason this book isn't exactly kid-friendly is its blatant racism. The dehumanizing references to squaws and half-breeds are one thing, but the real issue lies in the portrayal of the Yeehats.

The Yeehats, an invented tribe, are depicted as incompetent savages. They randomly kill Buck's beloved master, John Thornton, prompting Buck to seek revenge. Despite being a lone dog, he manages to attack and kill several of them. The Yeehats, armed and in a group, can't take down a single animal. They are such shitty hunters that they actually shoot each other in the battle. It's an absurd scenario that feeds into harmful stereotypes. The Yeehats are shown as barbaric and inferior, unable to match the prowess of the "white man's dog." Buck becomes a legend among them, a creature so formidable that the tribe fears him for years to come.

This portrayal reflects the colonial mindset of the time. London's depiction strips the Yeehats of complexity and humanity. They are mere obstacles for Buck to overcome, not real people with their own stories.

And then there's the machismo. The book drips with it. Buck isn't just a strong dog; he's the embodiment of rugged manliness, with constant references to his hard, rippling muscles. The emphasis on his physical strength, dominance, and aggression paints a clear picture of London's version of toxic masculinity.

The scenes of dogs tearing each other apart for weakness seem exaggerated. In reality, canine behavior is more nuanced. While dogs establish hierarchies, the savage brutality in *The Call of the Wild* is over the top. It's as if London wanted to amplify the idea that to survive, one must be relentlessly aggressive.

Wildness equates to masculinity here. The more Buck taps into his primal instincts, the more he embodies the ideal male. Domestication, on the other hand, is portrayed as weak and feminine.

Enter Mercedes, the most incompetent of the terrible trio. She's depicted as pathetic and annoying, a burden to the group. She's emotional, lazy, and out of touch with the harsh realities they face. Mercedes represents the peak of domestication and disconnection from the wild. Her character serves as a foil to Buck's ruggedness, highlighting the supposed shortcomings of femininity.

The idea that strength comes only from aggression and dominance is a narrow view that dismisses other forms of resilience and undermines the value of cooperation and empathy. So while *The Call of the Wild* can seem like a fun animal adventure on the surface, Buck the burly beast engages some themes and perspectives that are deserving of critique. That's not to say children shouldn't read it, but it's worth supplementing the story with some discussion about these problematic portrayals.

Why Is *The Call of the Wild* a Classic?

When *The Call of the Wild* was first published in 1903, it became an instant hit. Readers were drawn to Buck's gripping journey and London's vivid portrayal of the Yukon during the Gold Rush. But what has given this novel its staying power in American literature?

One key factor is the immersive quality of London's writing. His descriptions are rich and cinematic. You can feel the biting cold, hear the crunch of snow under paws, and sense the looming dangers of the wild: "He sat by John Thornton's fire, a broad-breasted dog, white-fanged and long-furred; but behind him were the shades of all manner of dogs, half-wolves, and wild wolves." The imagery here is powerful. It transports readers into the scene, bringing Buck's internal and external worlds to life.

Another reason the novel endures is its emotional draw. Buck starts as a loyal household dog, a creature many readers can relate to and whom many of us have loved. His ordeal is brutal, but with each stage of his transformation we witness his ability to adapt. We root for him because his struggle reflects a universal quest for survival, identity, and belonging.

Chapter Summary: It's a Dog's Life

The episodic structure of *The Call of the Wild* is a common feature in coming-of-age stories. This approach works when the protagonist has significant room for growth. Typically, a young protagonist has a lot to learn, and each episode marks a step in their development. In Buck's case, he's already a grown dog when the story begins, but he's as sheltered as a child. He has no idea what the real world is like. This structure serves the narrative (and thus the reader's experience) by allowing Buck to transform gradually. Each episode builds on the last, showing us not just a dog surviving one challenge after another, but a creature in the process of becoming.

Coming-of-Age: In coming-of-age narratives, the protagonist learns by moving through life and overcoming small challenges. A large part of the reader's emotional draw comes from witnessing these multiple character arcs. Each victory, no matter how small, feels powerful—because it is transformative. That's why this structure is harder to pull off in non-coming-of-age fiction, where the three-act structure dominates. In a typical three-act story, the character undergoes one main transformation while pursuing a challenging goal. Without a clear through-line, the plot can feel meandering.

Adult, YA, and MG Fiction: In today's literary market, books are categorized into adult, young adult, and middle grade fiction, each tailored to specific age groups and interests. Classics often fly in the face of these contemporary definitions.

- **Structure:** Adult novels often feature complex, multilayered plots with intricate subplots and complex themes. YA books typically have a faster pace with a focus on personal growth and self-discovery, centering on a clear narrative arc. MG fiction usually presents straightforward storytelling with a singular plotline, suitable for a younger readers.
- **Narrator Age:** Adult fiction can have protagonists of any age but often centers on adult characters. YA protagonists are generally aged 14 to 18, and MG protagonists are between 10 and 13. More specifically, fiction for young readers is typically marketed to certain age groups based on the

protagonist's age—usually the target age group for a novel is two years younger than the protagonist.
- **Length:** Adult novels vary widely but generally range from 70,000 to 120,000 words. YA novels are slightly shorter, averaging between 50,000 to 80,000 words, and MG books are shorter still, usually between 30,000 to 50,000 words.
- **Tone and Content:** Adult fiction delves into mature themes with sophisticated language and complex moral dilemmas. YA fiction tackles issues relevant to teenagers, such as identity, first love, and rebellion, using accessible language and an intimate tone. MG fiction addresses themes like friendship, family, and adventure, presented in a tone that balances seriousness with both humor and optimism.

Madame Bovary

by Gustave Flaubert

The Best Novel Ever Written?

High praise surrounds Gustave Flaubert's novel *Madame Bovary*. It has been called "perfect" by many great authors, a novel that approaches poetry, and "the best novel ever written." While Flaubert took five years to write it and famously labored over every word in his search for *le mot juste*, it's not only the language that hits the mark; it's also his realistic depiction of human nature.

The novel was controversial when it came out in 1857. Flaubert had to stand trial on obscenity charges on the grounds that the book promoted licentious behavior and undermined the institution of marriage—which makes us wonder if any of the authorities had actually read it. Flaubert was acquitted, arguing that the book depicted the consequences of immorality rather than endorsing it—which is exactly true.

By 1857, the Romantic movement in literature had seen its heyday. Flaubert rode the wave toward realism, a movement that aimed to show things in a more unadorned way. Together with Dickens, Balzac, and George Eliot, he is considered one of the founders of the genre of realism.

But there's a lot of irony in what he does here. He uses beautiful language to describe mediocrity and chooses a romantic character to reveal the tragic results of unbridled romanticism—and he does so with unflinching honesty. He blames Emma Bovary's tendency to romanticize life on the fact that she reads too many novels—while writing a novel about it.

Some people say this is a hard novel to read. It might be because none of the characters are likable, but it might also be because it hits a little too close to home. When Flaubert said, "*Madame Bovary, c'est moi*," what he really meant was that Madame Bovary is all of us. Her chronic dissatisfaction with life is humanity's default setting.

As a wife, Emma Bovary is your basic nightmare: she lives beyond her means, is perpetually unhappy, and cheats on her husband. She is the embodiment of wanting what you don't have and a fabulous illustration of the popular dictum *fuck around and find out*. She's a cautionary tale about the grass always being greener: never happy where she is, always imagining that other people are somehow having a better time than she is. One can almost imagine Mark Zuckerberg studying this novel as a template for Facebook.

Even though this is almost entirely Emma's story, it is bookended by Charles, her husband. She doesn't get a voice until she becomes Madame Bovary—as though she isn't worth listening to until she's married. But while it is her marriage to Charles that gives her a voice, that's not the event that sets her on the path to self-destruction.

Narrative Goal

Flaubert divides the novel into three parts.

- Part I: Charles meets and marries Emma, and they live in Tostes.
- Part II: They move to Yonville-l'Abbaye, and Emma meets Léon and Rodolphe.
- Part III: Emma renews her relationship with Léon, her life falls apart, and she commits suicide.

While there are two main characters—Charles and Emma—Emma is the clear protagonist. She's the one who has the significant narrative goal. But Flaubert is doing something interesting with goals. Charles gets what he wants quickly and then settles into a life of mediocrity, never really wanting anything—or rather, wanting what he already has. Emma, on the other hand, yearns for a life of wealth and excitement that she can never have as Madame Bovary, so she is doomed to perpetual dissatisfaction. Hers is a tragic trajectory. By the time she realizes that what she had was pretty good, it's too late.

Flaubert presents us with two choices: being happy with your lot even if it's mediocre or striving for a life you can never have, which causes you to be perpetually unhappy with what you do have.

Charles is the embodiment of mediocrity. He barely makes it through medical school and then works as an average provincial doctor. His first wife is chosen by his mother. The only desire he fashions for himself is to marry Emma, which he achieves early in the novel after his first wife dies. After that, he fades into the routine of daily life and has to be reminded to aspire to something greater—and when he does, it's a disaster.

While Emma does have a narrative goal (to live a life of wealth and glamour) this novel is a tragedy, so the action is driven more by her fatal flaw, which is to romanticize the lives of others and create perpetual dissatisfaction for herself. The reader doesn't really want to see her get what she wants, because we already know she will tire of it in due course. Instead, as in *The Picture of Dorian Gray*, we root for her to come to her senses. Her husband is at heart a good man, and she has a young daughter whom she consistently ignores—but a settled married life with a family is not in the cards for Emma.

So the trajectory in a nutshell is: When Emma attends a ball at a luxurious estate, she becomes dissatisfied with her lot and embarks on a series of adulterous affairs and out-of-control spending in an attempt to attain the life she glimpsed at that party. She must somehow find a way to stop this behavior, or she will lose her husband and daughter, the family's social standing, and all their belongings.

PLOT POINTS

Because the achievement of Charles' goal forms Emma's stasis, it's worth breaking down their two trajectories separately to see what Flaubert has done with the structure.

Charles' Narrative Trajectory

Part I begins with Charles as an average and somewhat ridiculous young man (stasis). He bumbles through his early years as a mama's boy, isn't especially smart or charming or good-looking, and marries a widow who is quite a bit older than he is but is purported to have money (although this turns out not to be true).

He receives a call in the middle of the night to set a farmer's broken leg—and that farmer is Emma's father. The first time we see Emma is through Charles' eyes (i.e., from the idealized perspective of an admirer). But while he flirts with her, he isn't free to pursue her (his goal) until his wife dies suddenly.

This death is his inciting incident because now his goal is achievable.

After his mourning period is over (rising action), he marries Emma—and reaches the climax of his trajectory. This resolution forms the beginning of Emma's stasis. Charles is set aside as the focal character, and Emma takes center stage.

Emma's Narrative Trajectory

Stasis and Inciting Incident

Already we get a glimpse of things to come when Emma wants a torchlit procession at midnight for her wedding but gets a feast in a cart-shed instead. Almost immediately, marriage does not live up to her romantic expectations. Charles' house needs repainting, the garden is scraggly, and all the things Emma read in romantic novels about love—bliss, passion, ecstasy—seem to be wrong. Marriage is just another in a series of life promises that fall short of what she imagined. So much for *happily ever after*.

But Emma's story doesn't swing into high gear until the couple receives an invitation to a ball at the mansion of the Marquis d'Andervilliers, one of Charles' patients. This is her inciting incident that allows her romantic motivation to develop into a goal. The enchanted evening gives Emma a glimpse of the kind of life she's read about in novels, and it makes her even more disillusioned by the circumstances she's stuck in—including the man she married. But she can still strive to live the storybook life she's dreamed of.

Rising Action

The more Emma thinks about this evening (and she fixates on it), the unhappier she becomes. She starts to measure time by its distance away from that night. She can't look at Charles the same way anymore. There's nothing inherently wrong with him. He's honest, hardworking, a good man. But he's bovine. He makes noise when he eats. He gains weight. There's no elegance about him. He's plodding.

Emma's unhappiness causes her to become so physically ill that Charles decides they should move elsewhere. And then she discovers she's pregnant. As she packs their things for the move, she finds her bridal bouquet and, in a significant and symbolic gesture, throws it into the fire.

The move to Yonville-l'Abbaye begins Part II of the novel and signals the advent of the next big dream for Emma. Maybe a change in location will be the thing to lift her life out of its dreadful boredom. Sure enough, when she meets Léon and discovers he too has an affinity for romantic novels, it seems like things might finally turn around. Over regular dinners at the house of Homais, the local apothecary, they develop an affinity for one another—to the point where people in town gossip that they're having an affair.

But as soon as Léon makes any move toward consummating this relationship, Emma steps away, embracing a romantic view of herself as a devoted wife and mother—a huge contradiction, seeing as how she barely communicates with either her husband or her child. She pretends to be thrifty but in fact craves luxury. When Lheureux, a shopkeeper in town, mentions that he can procure almost anything she might want and lend her money if she needs it, Flaubert plants a seed that will bear significant fruit as the novel progresses.

Eventually, Léon loses any hope of having a romantic relationship with Emma and leaves town.

Midpoint

After Léon leaves, the ennui of Emma's life becomes almost unbearable. She spends all her time daydreaming about him, but not quite him: "a taller, handsomer, a more delightful, and a vaguer Léon." She regrets not having taken up with him when she had the chance. She throws herself into trivialities—buys things from Lheureux, changes her hair, decides to learn Italian but doesn't pursue it.

Then Rodolphe Boulanger shows up, a wealthy landowner whose servant needs a doctor, and he is immediately smitten by Emma. He can see that she's bored. But unlike Léon, who was actually a decent person, Rodolphe is a charming but calculating con artist—the sort of man who wants what he can't have but then, once he gets it, tires of it quickly. As he plots how to seduce Emma, he's already wondering how he'll shake her off after he's had enough of her.

The scene at the agricultural fair when Rodolphe declares his love for Emma while an official is giving a speech about manure and pigs is masterful. Flaubert interweaves two separate strands of dialogue to create fabulous irony.

Flaubert has prepared the reader for Emma's colossal misstep at the midpoint. She spent so long pining over her missed chance with Léon, she's not going to mess it up this time. And indeed, Charles unwittingly facilitates the adultery by insisting she go riding with Rodolphe. She throws herself headlong into this affair, ignoring her family and buying luxurious things from Lheureux that she cannot afford. She idealizes Rodolphe into a man he most certainly is not and sets him up as the crutch in her life, the planet around which she orbits, the thing that makes her life worth living. But we know the truth about him. We know this relationship is doomed.

Rising Action

As expected, Rodolphe cools to Emma, and she begins to feel guilty about cheating on her husband. In an attempt to renew her commitment to Charles and boost his career, she encourages him to perform an extremely risky and unnecessary operation on Hippolyte, the stableman who was born with a clubfoot. If it succeeds, it will make Charles famous. Hippolyte manages just fine with his disability, but Homais and other townspeople push him into agreeing to the operation. It is an abject failure. Hippolyte develops gangrene, and his leg must be amputated. Instead of being famous,

Charles becomes infamous, which only reinforces Emma's opinion of him as incompetent.

She makes plans to take her daughter, Berthe, and run away with Rodolphe—which Rodolphe pretends to be on board with. But at the last minute he writes her a letter breaking off their affair. When she sees his carriage drive off, she becomes so ill she nearly dies. In order to pay for her consultations with specialists, Charles must borrow money from Lheureux at a high rate of interest.

When Emma finally recovers, she throws herself into Catholicism. This is familiar territory for her. She went to convent school as a teenager and romanticizes that period in her life. Naturally, it doesn't live up to her impossible and idealized expectations. Homais suggests Charles should take Emma to the opera in Rouen to make her feel better, and he does. Once again, ironically, it is Charles who facilitates her next affair.

We move into Part III of the novel, where Emma bumps into Léon at the opera and their feelings for each other are rekindled. So much for Catholicism. Emma makes a lame attempt to resist him by writing a letter explaining why she can't have an affair with him, but that goes out the window (literally) when they hire a carriage to drive them around all day and stay in the back with the drapes drawn.

But Flaubert is busy planting more seeds, reminding us that any possibility of victory in this story will be false and short-lived. When Emma returns to Yonville, there is death and there are debts. Charles' father has died; Homais and his assistant, Justin, have a huge argument because Justin has taken the key to the storeroom where the arsenic is kept; and Lheureux comes around looking for money to settle what is becoming an alarmingly long list of debts.

Emma becomes obsessed with Léon in much the same way she did with Rodolphe, setting him up as the center of her life. But the romance with Léon soon loses its initial spark—as romances are wont to do—and Emma "[rediscovers] in adultery all the banalities of marriage." Boom. The novel is worth reading for that line alone.

Léon is a disappointment. And here is the crux of her (and humanity's) existential dilemma: "What caused this inadequacy in her life? Why did everything she leaned on instantaneously decay? … There was nothing that was worth going far to get: all was lies! Every smile concealed a yawn of boredom, every joy a misery. Every pleasure brought its surfeit; and the loveliest kisses only left upon your lips a baffled longing for a more intense delight."

She has had erotic bliss and luxuries, and—surprise (no surprise)—they turn out to be insufficient. Could it be that plodding, ordinary Charles has had the answer all along? Emma, however, is not blessed with that kind of insight. Instead, Lheureux talks her into borrowing more money, because surely money will solve everything.

A Brief False Victory

Eventually a debt collector shows up and things become dire. Emma borrows more money from Lheureux and sells her old gloves and hats and other household items, but it's not enough. A court order arrives, stating that she must come up with an exorbitant sum or the family will lose everything. In desperation, she turns to Rodolphe for help—to the point of offering herself in exchange for money—and it almost seems like he might help her. It's undoubtedly the case that he *could*. But that's it for the glimmer of false victory: he doesn't.

Emma's daydreams and romantic illusions have officially come crashing down around her. *Fuck around and find out* indeed.

Tragic Climax

At her wits' end, Emma goes to the apothecary, where she begs Justin to open the storeroom for her. Without really thinking it through, she shovels a bunch of arsenic into her mouth and imagines she will swoon into a peaceful death the way all tragic heroines do. But that is not the way one dies from arsenic. Committed to realism right to the end, Flaubert shows us the gruesome reality of such a death. It's awful, and there's nothing anyone can do except watch her suffer.

Resolution

Charles' devastation at Emma's death is part of the tragedy at the end. He loved her. He never suspected her of having an affair. Even when he finds Rodolphe's last letter, he thinks the best of her. But this, too, is a form of illusion.

The story shifts mostly back to Charles as he lives through the wreckage that Emma left behind. There are still creditors. The way Emma lived has ruined Charles financially. When at last he discovers all the letters exchanged between Emma and both Léon and Rodolphe, he can no longer deny reality. He dies shortly afterward, and poor Berthe, now an orphan, gets passed on to various relatives before ending up working in a cotton mill.

Life goes on. Emma fades away, and the book ends with the success of Homais, the apothecary—the character who most fully symbolizes the bourgeoisie in the novel. *Vive la médiocrité*. One can only admire Flaubert for his commitment to harsh reality right to the end.

What's in a Name?

Flaubert's choice of the name Bovary is no accident. Charles is like a cow, the most mediocre animal imaginable. The fact that Emma acquires the name Bovary when what she wants is an extraordinary and sophisticated life only heightens the irony that abounds in this novel. She is doomed to disillusionment, doomed to navigate the abyss between the life she desires and the one she's stuck with.

What's also interesting is the way Flaubert moves between referring to his protagonist as Emma or Madame Bovary. The title of Madame reminds the reader that Emma is married (since she seems to forget rather frequently). It is her formal position in society and a key source of her unhappiness. It also becomes ironic depending on where it appears. Her proper name, Emma, is more intimate.

The fact that the title of the book is *Madame Bovary* and not Emma Bovary is also significant. Emma's marriage (and perhaps marriage in general) is where romantic fantasy does battle with harsh reality.

Point of View

One of the many things that makes this novel noteworthy is what Flaubert does with point of view and how he manages to make us willing to follow his unlikable characters to the end.

Take whatever you thought you knew about point of view and throw it out the window. Flaubert does largely what he wants in this novel. He begins with the plural "we" to show Charles from the perspective of his classmates. The novel then shifts to an omniscient voice. Readers remain more or less in Charles' head until he marries Emma, and then the novel shifts to show us the world mostly through Emma's eyes. But not entirely. Flaubert moves around when it suits him. Sometimes the voice is objective, but he often uses free indirect discourse (as Jane Austen does in *Pride and Prejudice*) to deliver Emma's thoughts and feelings. He varies the tone depending on her mood. He captures the pomposity of Homais, a character who embodies everything about the bourgeoisie that Flaubert despised. He shows us the calculated scheming of Rodolphe.

Mostly the author seems to sympathize with Emma's plight, but there are many times in the novel where it seems like he hates his characters. In 1857, he wrote to Leroyer de Chantepie that he did not intend to give his own opinion about any of them: "The artist must be in his work as God is in creation, invisible and all-powerful; one must sense him everywhere but never see him." But it comes through, nonetheless.

Flaubert uses point of view as a sharp and manipulative tool (which is what it is) to keep readers on their toes. He doesn't make this easy. We're not allowed to hate Charles without also feeling sorry for him. We're not allowed to scorn Emma without also recognizing ourselves in her, at least to some extent. We're not allowed to turn up our noses at mediocrity without also realizing that Emma could have had a pretty good life if she'd accepted it, that she was a crap wife and a crap mother—but can we really blame her for rejecting mediocrity and wanting something more? No, we can't. Rodolphe's rejection of her is heartbreaking. Emma's financial desperation is full of tension. Her suicide is horrific. We are fully engaged with this deeply flawed character even though she leaves both chaos and financial ruin in her wake.

Why Is *Madame Bovary* a Classic?

"I have just spent a good week," Flaubert wrote to a friend while he was working on *Madame Bovary*, "alone like a hermit and calm as a god. I abandoned myself to a frenzy of literature. I got up at midday, I went to bed at four in the morning; I have written eight pages."

What author cannot relate to this sentiment? The struggle is real. But it is also one of the reasons this novel has endured for so long. The language is stunning. Flaubert's hard work paid off. But *Madame Bovary* also endures because of how deeply human his characters are.

Flaubert doesn't shy away from human emotion at its worst. We see ourselves in Emma whether we want to or not. Her tragedy—that she cannot be content with what she has—is what our entire consumer society is built upon. Her illusions of what other people's airbrushed lives are like form the beating heart of social media, magazines, romance novels, and Hollywood.

No wonder the novel still resonates.

Chapter Summary: Unhappily Ever After

Flaubert breaks a lot of rules in *Madame Bovary*, but he does so intentionally to serve the story. He allows one character to achieve their narrative goal early and uses it as a springboard for the main character to be perpetually dissatisfied. He wields POV like a sharp weapon, inserting the knife wherever necessary to achieve the effects he's after. Most impressive of all, he creates emotional draw even with characters that aren't likable.

Le Mot Juste: This French phrase translates to "the exact right word." It embodies a writer's pursuit of linguistic precision and perfection, aiming to choose words that most accurately and effectively convey the intended meaning, emotion, or nuance. Gustave Flaubert is renowned for his dedication to *le mot juste*. He meticulously crafted his sentences, often spending considerable time refining his prose to achieve absolute clarity and expressiveness. This commitment to precision enhances the realism and depth of his work, allowing readers to fully immerse themselves in the characters' experiences. Flaubert's emphasis on *le mot juste* has influenced countless writers and remains a cornerstone concept in literary craftsmanship.

An Unlikable Protagonist: In *Madame Bovary*, Flaubert proves that a strong protagonist doesn't have to be likable. But they do have to be intriguing in some way; interesting enough that we are drawn to them in the way we're drawn to a traffic accident. We can't look away. Part of the emotional draw of a deeply flawed character is their believability. We know people like this. We even see glimmers of ourselves in the character. But it's also the way we as readers invest ourselves in the outcome of this flawed character's fate. We root for them to find a way out of their terrible predicament. We cheer their victories and hope that they stick (though, of course, they don't).

Flaubert also invests Emma with a universal desire: she wants a better life. She sees the green grass on the other side of the fence and believes it is better than the patch of lawn she stands on. This creates strong relatability. The result is that even if we are unlike Emma in many ways, there will be some aspects of her character that we can't help but sympathize with.

Keeping it Real: Flaubert's commitment to realism is admirable, even when it means he has to be hard on his characters. There were many places where he could have stepped back and gone easier on poor Emma. It's a common tendency among authors to shy away from conflict and not make the worst thing happen. Who wants to see their beloved characters suffer? But Flaubert resists this temptation. Even at the end, we see Emma's death from arsenic poisoning in all its gruesome detail.

Heart of Darkness

by Joseph Conrad

The Scramble for Africa

Heart of Darkness is an 1899 novella written by the Polish-British author Joseph Conrad. It's a fascinating exploration not only of European colonialism in Africa (the Scramble for Africa, it was called) but also a wonderful illustration of how authors can use both concepts and imagery to imply their opposite: tackling darkness by bringing the (supposed) light of civilization.

Not only was Conrad born in a country that has repeatedly been carved up by other nations (Poland), but he also traveled to the Congo as a young man, serving on one of the Belgian trading company's steamers, much like the protagonist, Charlie Marlow.

While many have argued about who the prototype for Kurtz—the corrupted ivory trader Marlow seeks—might have been, no one can refute the brutality of what happened in Africa when the Europeans arrived. This is a shocking book that forces readers, settlers in particular, to do some serious thinking about the nature of civilization: "The conquest of the earth, which mostly means the taking it away from those who have a different complexion or slightly flatter noses than ourselves, is not a pretty thing when you look into it too much. What redeems it is the idea only... something you can set up, and bow down before, and offer a sacrifice to."

And of course, what Conrad really means is that it is irredeemable. There is no higher ideal in operation here. Kurtz, the man who "enlarges people's minds" sets himself up as a god to be worshipped; what starts as a humanitarian endeavor ends as a self-aggrandizing disaster.

This book operates almost entirely on irony. Marlow begins by contrasting colonists with conquerors, but in the story he goes on to tell, there's no doubt that the colonists behave like conquerors—their strength comes from the subjugation of others. They grab what they can, simply because it's there and they've got the bigger guns: "It was just robbery with violence, aggravated murder on a great scale, and men going at it blind—as is very proper for those who tackle a darkness."

It's the light that brings the horror to the Congo: European colonialism. The heart of darkness is not at the center of Africa at all. It's within us.

Narrative Goal

Heart of Darkness is written as a traditional seaman's yarn. Five men are on board the *Nellie*, a boat on the Thames, waiting for the tide to turn—the captain plus four others, only one of whom is named: the lawyer, the accountant, the narrator, and Marlow. They have to pass the time somehow, so Marlow decides to tell them his story.

While the narrator's voice bookends the novella, the story itself belongs to Marlow, making this a frame narrative. Conrad keeps the voice conversational as he shows Marlow's slow but steady realization of the truth that he encounters in the Congo. Here again, the use of light and darkness is skillfully employed. Marlow's eyes are slowly opened—as are ours. This is a journey from innocence to experience for both Marlow and the reader.

Using the oral tradition creates a nice echo of storytelling cultures, another in a series of ironies. But that's not the only reason Conrad has chosen it. The narrator's opinions about London's exalted place in the world and humanity's right to assert dominion over nature are about to be challenged. Because, regardless of what they claimed, the Belgian trading company was not about bringing light (progress) to the dark (uncivilized) places of the world. They were after ivory.

However, it is also worth considering that Marlow might be an unreliable narrator. After all, he's the only one who comes out of this story looking somewhat decent. It forces readers to question how much of what he tells us is what really happened and how much he has spun to make himself look good. It also allows Conrad to place distance between himself and his narrator so that the reader doesn't confuse Marlow's views with those of the author.

On the surface, Marlow's story is quite simple. He accepts a job traveling along the Congo River, first to retrieve the bones of his predecessor but eventually to fetch a renowned ivory trader named Kurtz and bring him home. But the farther he travels into the "heart of darkness," the more he hears stories and rumors about Kurtz. The whole novella soon centers on the character of Kurtz, whom the reader doesn't meet until near the end.

Kurtz has apparently gone to the Congo to bring the light of European civilization to the dark heart of Africa, though he is incidentally also the best agent the company has ever had—"best" being measured by how much ivory he brings in. Over time, whatever civilization he brings breaks down into egomania and savagery (his). On the journey to find Kurtz, Marlow becomes obsessed with him. What began as a desire for adventure turns into a battle for Marlow to hold on to his moral compass. He must retrieve Kurtz while also coming to terms with both the corrupting force of power and the realities of colonialism.

PLOT POINTS

Structurally, Marlow's story follows Joseph Campbell's hero's journey. When we bring in some of the typical archetypes associated with the hero's journey, it illuminates Marlow's relationship with Kurtz in a way that makes more sense than the traditional protagonist/antagonist dichotomy.

The frame story sets up the hero's journey: five men are on a boat on the Thames waiting for the tide to turn. When the narrator makes a statement about the great civilized city of London, Marlow watches the sun set and imagines what the Romans must have thought when they first arrived here to bring civilization to this part of the world. As darkness settles on the river, he says, "This also has been one of the dark places of the earth." He then proceeds to show us how.

Departure (Act One)

In the first part of the hero's journey, the hero receives a call to adventure, leaves their home, and embarks on a quest. (Since Joseph Cambell uses different plot-point terms, we've put them in bold below for clarity.)

After extensive travel, Marlow, a ship's captain, has returned to London—a pinnacle of European civilization and colonial ambition—and decides to pursue his lifelong desire to explore Africa. When he realizes there is a company that trades on the Congo River, he finds a job with them piloting a steamboat. This is his **call to adventure**, the catalyst that will take him away from his familiar world and into the unknown. But the actual inciting incident will come later.

It's worth mentioning here that while the catalyst and inciting incident are often interchangeable structural terms, this is not always the case. Sometimes, like here, the catalyst gets the story moving and sends the protagonist in a new direction, but their true quest—which crystallizes in the inciting incident—doesn't materialize until later.

Hero's journey stories often also include a **refusal of the call**. After saying goodbye to his aunt, Marlow expresses a sudden reluctance to undertake the journey, a moment "I won't say of hesitation, but of startled pause ... as though, instead of going to the center of a continent, I were about to set off for the center of the earth."

But it's only a moment, and off he goes on a French steamer, sailing along the African coastline to the Company's first station. It is here where he can truly be said to **cross the threshold** into the new world. This is where he first sees people chained to each other: criminals, supposedly—though they look a lot like slaves. He also sees holes being dug for no reason, smashed drainpipes, and a railway that isn't getting built. It is his first snapshot of the lie of civilization and progress.

His initial task is to retrieve the body of a steamer captain (the one he's replacing) who was killed in an argument with the natives over some hens. At the station, he meets the Company's chief accountant, a **mentor** of sorts. This is the first person to mention Mr. Kurtz to Marlow—a "remarkable" person and "first-class agent," who sends in as much ivory as all the other agents put together. At that point, Marlow sets off on a two-hundred-mile trek to the central station to fetch his steamer. But the task of picking up Kurtz has not yet been broached.

Initiation (Act Two)

This section of the hero's journey usually corresponds to the part of a traditional three-act structure that spans everything from rising action to the midpoint and climax of the story. It begins with **tests, allies, and enemies.**

Marlow's first test occurs when he discovers that the boat he was supposed to pilot is sitting at the bottom of the river and will need to be pulled out and repaired. He meets the Manager, an ordinary-looking man who embodies Hannah Arendt's concept of the banality of evil. There's nothing remarkable about him other than that he has the stomach for this place (most who come there do not). At first it's hard to say if the Manager is an ally, mentor, or enemy, but irony is at work here as well. He should be an ally and mentor, but as a Company man, he symbolizes everything that is terrible about colonialism: the exploitation, greed, and indifference to human suffering.

It's the Manager who gives Marlow his quest and enlists him in fetching Kurtz (at last, here is the inciting incident, unusually late). The job of retrieving Kurtz is apparently how the boat was wrecked in the first place: Kurtz has become very ill, and the Manager took it out in a hurry and hit some rocks.

Over the months it takes Marlow to repair the boat, he meets the Brickmaker, though he never sees him make any bricks. And he hears lots more about Kurtz. When the boat is finally ready, he heads up the river with the Manager and a group of cannibals—which seems like an odd choice for shipmates until one realizes that the cannibals have more humanity than the Manager.

Marlow explores a hut on the riverbank that contains a woodpile with a sign in English saying that the wood is for him and that he should hurry. In the hut he finds an English book—a strange test.

Fog on the river delays them. When it rises and they proceed to a narrower part of the channel, hostile natives attack them with arrows and the helmsman is killed. There is a sense that Marlow is traveling into a surreal world, though he starts to think Kurtz must be dead and regrets that he won't get the chance to meet him.

After two months they reach Kurtz's trading station, which represents the **inmost cave**, the deepest point of darkness. Marlow meets the Russian, an agent with the Dutch trading company who's been on the river for two years. He's the one who left them the wood.

He says the locals attacked them because they were afraid Marlow was coming to take Kurtz away (which he is).

The trading station is surrounded by stakes topped with round orbs that Marlow soon realizes are heads—the heads of rebels, according to Kurtz. He finds out that the tribe Kurtz is living with treats him like a god. Things are not good here. Kurtz has clearly become unstable.

When the Manager and other men return with Kurtz, he's on a makeshift stretcher and is very ill. During the **supreme ordeal** (the climax in three-act structure), Marlow finally meets him face-to-face. In the middle of the night, Kurtz makes his escape on all fours. Marlow tracks him down, though they are now near a native camp. One word from Kurtz, and Marlow could be killed.

In a **seizing the sword** moment (the moment of **transformation**), Marlow stares into his shadow self and realizes that whatever is inside Kurtz is also in him—that all humans are capable of both evil and goodness in equal measure, and that to judge someone by any other standards is to fall prey to hypocrisy.

Return (Act Three)

The return is essentially an extended version of three-act structure's resolution. In this last section of the hero's journey, the hero returns home, bringing something that will help the community, thanks to the experiences they had and the wisdom they gained.

The road back along the river toward civilization is twice as fast, though the life is also ebbing from Kurtz, and Marlow himself becomes ill. Kurtz entrusts Marlow with his papers, suggesting that Marlow is an heir in some way to his legacy. Marlow is the only one present to hear Kurtz's last words: "The horror, the horror."

Entire PhDs have no doubt been written about that moment. What does it mean? Conrad doesn't tell us. There have been so many surreal and even absurd moments on this journey that he might be suggesting this whole money grab disguised as humanitarianism is also absurd—and intrinsically horrific. But it might also mean that no one can exempt themselves from the possibility of moral depravity. We are each of us capable of anything.

In any case, Marlow himself is so ill, he nearly dies. His **resurrection** in Brussels is both physical and spiritual. He returns with a new understanding of the human condition (and his own soul), as well as the dangers of unchecked power. But he also protects Kurtz's widow from the darkness he has glimpsed. She is still blinded by her admiration of the man. When she asks about Kurtz's last words, Marlow lies and says Kurtz spoke her name.

We return to the framing device, where the men have been sitting on the *Nellie* listening to Marlow's story. This is the **elixir** that he has returned with—he has recounted his experiences to them. The original narrator now stares toward London, which appears to be at "the heart of an immense darkness." The reversal that Marlow insisted upon at the beginning has now been achieved. The narrator realizes that his assumptions about colonialism have been misguided. The hero's journey is complete.

The Archetypes

Rather than thinking of Kurtz as an antagonist—because he isn't exactly working against Marlow—it is more helpful to think of him as Marlow's **shadow**. In a story that is built on the imagery of light and darkness, he is Marlow's opposite. He embodies the impulses Marlow must fight against within himself.

Marlow arrives in the Congo expecting to see colonialism as it has been billed: the bringer of progress and civilization. What he discovers is a place where the French shoot blindly into the jungle, the brickmaker doesn't make bricks, Marlow's steamer ship sits at the bottom of the river, and holes are dug for no reason. At the center of this fiasco is Kurtz, the one everyone thinks of as a god. The one who sees himself as a "supernatural being" deserving of worship, who is said to be a great humanitarian and yet recommends at the end of his report on the "suppression of savage customs" that they "exterminate all the brutes." He arrives in Africa as a force of light but finishes as a source of darkness. Marlow must fight against being drawn into this vortex.

The Africans themselves are the **shapeshifters** in this story. When Marlow first sees them in chains, he thinks they are criminals. They've been described to him as enemies. Then he sees the starving and diseased mine workers—neither criminals nor enemies. In both cases, they appear more like slaves. When at last Marlow encounters the heads on stakes at Kurtz's house—supposedly the heads of rebels—he says, "What would be the next definition I was to hear? There had been enemies, criminals, workers—and these were rebels." No one calls them what they really are: the victims of uncontrolled greed.

There are various **allies** in the book, people from the trading company who are ostensibly on Marlow's side to help him in his quest to track down Kurtz, though none of them really behaves as an ally. The Manager seems sketchy and makes everyone uneasy. The Russian Trader is unbalanced in his fervent devotion to Kurtz. His patched, jester-like clothing almost suggests a **trickster** figure, but he is more fool than wise man.

The Power of Foreshadowing

Heart of Darkness is a master class in how to prepare an audience for a character who doesn't appear until near the end. Conrad allows other characters to mention Kurtz—over and over. He is controversial. The best agent ever. He is ill. He's a demigod. One must listen to him. One must meet him. He is eloquent. He is evil. He embodies the rapacious greed of Europe.

In fact, Kurtz seems to be whatever others want him to be. Later, Marlow is surprised to discover Kurtz is a talented musician—or was, before he lost his way. His widow seems utterly bewitched by his capacity for goodness. The one thing he is not is someone we can ignore.

By the time we finally meet Kurtz in person, we have been prepared. This is a man who has people bowing down to him, a man who mounts the heads of those who don't agree with him on stakes and sets them around his home where he can see them. Even though he is sick and dying by the time Marlow encounters him, he still has the strength of will to crawl into the jungle to prevent Marlow from taking him home.

Danger in general is foreshadowed by Conrad's keen attention to detail. The river is referred to repeatedly as a snake. Fog creates a feeling of both claustrophobia and unseen threat; the jungle thickens, and there are eyes in the bushes. The river narrows, and the steamer chugs on, deeper into the heart of darkness. And everything leads to Kurtz.

There's also a scene early in the novella that seems innocent but is full of menace. Before Marlow leaves on his journey, he must be seen by a doctor who wants to measure his head and asks if madness runs in the family. He sees everyone who leaves for Africa, but he never sees them when they come back. If they come back.

Why Is *Heart of Darkness* a Classic?

According to the literary critic Harold Bloom, *Heart of Darkness* is the most frequently analyzed work of literature in universities and colleges, probably because Conrad doesn't spell things out for his readers. He leaves the door so wide open for interpretation that it makes the book quite inhospitable to the reader. It's hard to get into and hard to push through.

It's worth remembering that this novella came out in 1899 as a serial and in 1902 in book form. Conrad's view of Western progress would have been unpopular—and indeed the novella was not a huge success. He was one of the first to question both the notion that Europeans had cornered the market on civilization and progress, and to condemn colonialism.

However, the novella has been lambasted by authors like Chinua Achebe for being racist and promoting a prejudiced and dehumanized view of Africa. This is undeniably true. At one point, Marlow even suggests the Africans have a hint of tails. Africa is portrayed as uncivilized and populated by people who are less than human. But is this Conrad's view or Marlow's? Conrad might have chosen a frame narrative for this very reason: so that readers do not conflate his opinion with that of Marlow (i.e., the prevailing worldview).

Certainly, Conrad could have criticized colonialism in a way that didn't also promote both racism and harmful stereotypes. It would be an interesting exercise to consider how the book would be different if he'd done that. But maybe, given the time and place, European views were not sufficiently advanced for him to write that kind of book. It lands with more of a tone-deaf thump now, but it also forces the reader to engage with difficult subject matter and consider how much has changed—and how much still remains to be done.

Despite the book's limitations, Conrad took a brave stand against colonialism and the flow of so-called progress and said what few others were willing to say. In the end, he seems to cast a vote for the cleansing power of nature. While the Europeans with their "imbecile rapacity" seem to be praying to ivory, "outside, the silent wilderness ... struck me as something great and invincible ... waiting patiently for the passing away of this fantastic invasion."

Conrad grasped something essential about the nature and stupidity of human greed that is sadly still relevant today.

Chapter Summary: Into the Abyss

Conrad employs the hero's journey structure, which in itself would be simple, but he also employs a frame narrative that allows for the possibility of an unreliable narrator and creates distance between the narrator and himself. A delayed inciting incident makes the structure harder to pin down. *Heart of Darkness* is notable for its motifs of light and darkness and how Conrad uses them ironically in order to reinforce the theme. It's also a good novella to study for anyone who wants to delay the arrival of a major character.

Frame Narrative: A frame narrative is a storytelling technique where a main story is encased within another story—a narrative within a narrative. This outer story sets the context, providing a frame for the inner narrative and often offering additional perspectives or commentary. The frame can serve to distance the author from the events, introduce unreliable narrators, or create layers of meaning.

In *Heart of Darkness*, Joseph Conrad employs a frame narrative by beginning and ending the novella with an unnamed narrator aboard the ship *Nellie* on the Thames River. This narrator listens as Charles Marlow recounts his journey into the Congo. The use of this frame allows Conrad to create a sense of storytelling intimacy and to highlight the themes of perception and truth. It also introduces the possibility of an unreliable narrator, as readers receive Marlow's account filtered through another's perspective, adding complexity to the interpretation of events and characters like Kurtz.

Inciting Incident Versus Catalyst: The catalyst and the inciting incident are often one and the same, but that's not always the case. The catalyst is an event that initiates the story, propelling the protagonist out of their normal life and setting the stage for the main action. The inciting incident, on the other hand, is the specific event where the protagonist's primary goal becomes clear.

In this case, the catalyst is Marlow's decision to take a job with a Belgian trading company to captain a steamboat in Africa. This event sets him on his journey but doesn't yet define his primary goal. The inciting incident occurs later when Marlow arrives at the central station and learns about Kurtz's troubling situation. He is then tasked with retrieving Kurtz, which cements his narrative goal. The split between the catalyst and the late inciting incident allows Conrad to immerse readers in the unsettling atmosphere of colonial Africa and to build suspense around the enigmatic figure of Kurtz. It also allows for Marlow's gradual awakening to the realities of imperialism and the moral complexities he will face.

Foreshadowing: Joseph Conrad uses foreshadowing extensively to evoke a sense of impending doom and to underscore the novella's central themes. Examples include:

- **The doctor's warning:** Before Marlow departs, a doctor measures his skull and remarks on the mental changes that may occur in those who venture into the Congo, hinting at the psychological turmoil Marlow will experience.
- **The dark imagery of the river:** The Congo River is repeatedly described with ominous metaphors, such as a "snake uncoiled," symbolizing the danger and temptation that lie ahead.

- **The wrecked steamer:** Marlow's steamboat is found sunk and in disrepair, foreshadowing the obstacles and chaos he will encounter on his mission.
- **Whispers about Kurtz:** Early references to Kurtz as a remarkable yet enigmatic figure build intrigue and hint at his ultimate moral decay.

Foreshadowing allows you to get away with things like plot twists and events or behavior that would otherwise strain credulity. When you plant clues for the reader, you lay the groundwork for future events, thereby preventing your plot from feeling contrived or coincidental. You can also use foreshadowing as a form of misdirection (the way Charlotte Brontë does in *Jane Eyre* with the character of Blanche Ingram). The key is in the amount that you use: not enough and you create confusion; too much and you risk predictability.

Joseph Campbell's Hero's Journey: The hero's journey, also known as the monomyth, is a narrative pattern identified by mythologist Joseph Campbell in his seminal work, *The Hero with a Thousand Faces* (1949). Campbell studied myths from various cultures and discovered a common structure underlying many heroic tales, consisting of stages that a protagonist typically experiences on their journey.

The hero's journey is divided into three main acts:

- **Departure (Separation):** The hero begins in the ordinary world and receives a call to adventure. Initially they may refuse the call, but eventually they cross the threshold into the unknown.
- **Initiation:** The hero faces trials, encounters allies and enemies, and undergoes significant challenges, including a central ordeal. This act culminates in a personal transformation.

- **Return:** After overcoming the ordeal, the hero returns to the ordinary world with new knowledge, wisdom, or an elixir that benefits others.

Campbell's framework has had a profound impact on modern storytelling, influencing writers and creators across various media. But it's important to acknowledge that while many stories align with the hero's journey plot points, authors may not intentionally design their narratives around this structure. Instead, the monomyth represents archetypal patterns that naturally emerge in storytelling.

Part Three: Cracking the Code

Quite often when we first broach the topic of structural elements in a writing workshop, someone will ask: isn't three-act structure formulaic? It seems like it could be. The same old inciting incident and rising action, same old midpoint and climax. Boring. Right?

If that's what you're thinking, then hold on to your hat. These next novels offer readers a wild structural ride. They are the ones that challenged us the most, kept us awake at night, made us return to the text over and over to figure out what the authors were doing. They show the incredible creative potential contained in narrative structure.

Formulaic? Perish the thought! We'll show you genre mash-ups, dizzying arrays of narrative goals and storylines, and an entire cast of unreliable narrators. There's one novel that doesn't seem to have a plot (oh, but it does!) and another that doesn't seem to have a protagonist (yes, there is one). Event structures, Venn diagrams—these classic authors prove just how flexible three-act structure can be.

Jane Eyre
by Charlotte Brontë

A Classic Structural Mash-Up

Jane Eyre is an important novel in the English literature canon for several reasons. At the time it was written, it was groundbreaking in terms of challenging the female norm, which was to be submissive and quiet. Jane Austen's novels were all about marrying well, and then here comes Jane Eyre: outspoken, headstrong, and defiant. Her desire for independence is a significant aspect of her personality. Throughout the novel, she struggles to maintain her integrity while repeatedly coming up against people in positions of power who make her feel inferior.

For a novel that features one of the few strong female protagonists in Victorian literature, it's ironic that the author, Charlotte Brontë, had to publish it under a male pseudonym (Currer Bell).

The book is divided into three volumes, which was a common way to publish a novel in the nineteenth century. But its structure is surprisingly complex. In terms of genre, it straddles both bildungsroman (coming-of-age) and gothic romance. Written in first person as a fictional autobiography, it traces Jane's development from childhood through to adulthood, from innocence to maturity. But Jane's romance with Mr. Rochester dominates three-quarters of the novel, which skews the typically episodic bildungsroman structure.

Some critics contend that the entire first quarter of the novel is "unnecessary" and that the real story only begins when Jane goes to work for Mr. Rochester. If the novel were purely a gothic romance, this would be a valid point. But the first part of the novel also establishes Jane's core misbelief—that she is unworthy of love—and underscores the coming-of-age aspect of the book. Jane wants independence, which is typical of a bildungsroman protagonist. But what she needs is love—thus fulfilling the goal of the romance genre.

For our purposes, it's more helpful to divide the novel into five sections, each with its own arc.

Setting as Structure

Setting is the key organizational tool in *Jane Eyre*. There are five main settings: Gateshead Hall, Lowood School, Thornfield Hall, Moor House, and Ferndean. Each one corresponds to a different stage of Jane's maturity: childhood, adolescence, young adulthood, adulthood, and married life. Each one gives physicality to her struggle for independence.

PLOT POINTS

Gateshead Hall: Coming-Of-Age Stage One

Jane, an orphan, is sent to live at Gateshead Hall with the Reeds, wealthy relatives who never let her forget she's the poor relation who will never amount to anything (stasis). Jane's initial goal is simple: to be treated like an equal.

When the Reeds' son, John, physically mistreats Jane yet again (inciting incident), she fights back and is locked in the Red Room—the room where her beloved uncle was laid out after he passed away. Despondent and afraid, she has a vision of his ghost and is severely traumatized (rising action). Even though this moment cements the realization of her powerlessness as an orphan, it also turns out to be the path away from the Reeds. It is at this stage that

Jane's goal changes (midpoint reversal). She realizes she will never be treated like one of the Reed children. The only way she can survive is to leave.

Mr. Brocklehurst, the head of Lowood School, arranges for Jane to attend his girls' boarding school (climax). Before leaving, Jane tells Mrs. Reed what she thinks of her, cementing both her outspoken personality and the family's rejection of her (semi-resolution).

Lowood School: Coming-Of-Age Stage Two

Lowood School turns out to be dismal and poorly funded, with not enough food or heat (stasis). Several girls fall ill with typhus and some die, including Jane's dear friend Helen (inciting incident), but Jane perseveres and survives. Because she cannot rely on family for help, education becomes her path to independence. Her goal in this section is to do well at school so that she can make a life for herself while also maintaining her dignity.

Jane graduates and becomes a teacher at the school (rising action), but when her favorite teacher leaves to get married, she realizes it's time for a change (climax). In a significant move toward independence, she accepts a position as governess at Thornfield Manor to a young girl named Adele (semi-resolution).

Thornfield Hall: Love, but Not Independence

Jane settles in nicely to life at Thornfield Hall (stasis) and then meets Mr. Rochester when his horse slips on some ice (inciting incident). At first, he seems cold and pretentious, but they soon warm to each other and spend many evenings together talking. When Jane saves Mr. Rochester from a mysterious fire in his bedroom (rising action), it becomes clear that they're falling in love, and she dares to imagine a life with him.

This relationship is challenged by the arrival of Blanche Ingram, who is haughty, beautiful, and shallow (midpoint). This is simultaneously an all-is-lost moment since Jane's goal of marrying Mr. Rochester now seems impossible. She assumes Mr. Rochester and Blanche will get married even though they don't act like they're in love. Once again, Jane is reminded of her powerlessness as a member of the lower class. Blanche treats her exactly the way Mrs. Reed treated her—like trash.

When Mrs. Reed takes ill, Jane returns to Gateshead Hall to see her (rising action). There is resolution of this storyline and a certain poetic justice in discovering the members of the Reed family have not fared well. On her deathbed, Mrs. Reed reveals that Jane has an uncle in Madeira who wanted to adopt her and bequeath her money, but Mrs. Reed told him Jane was dead. While Jane's aunt still can't get over her enmity toward Jane, Jane shows admirable mercy and forgiveness toward her aunt.

Jane returns to Thornfield expecting to learn of Mr. Rochester's marriage to Blanche. Instead, he proposes to her, and she accepts (false victory). While Mr. Rochester does not treat Jane like trash, the reader can't help but wonder about the power and class differential between them. Mr. Rochester offers love, but Jane will have to compromise her independence to accept it.

At the wedding ceremony, a man announces that Mr. Rochester cannot marry Jane because he's already married… to a madwoman named Bertha (tragic climax). Mr. Rochester offers to whisk Jane away to the mainland where they can live in sin, but Jane refuses to compromise her principles. Early the next morning, she steals away, breaking both her own heart and Rochester's (semi-resolution).

Moor House: Independence, but Not Love

Jane wanders without food or shelter for several days (stasis) and is finally taken in at Moor House by apparent strangers: St. John Rivers and his sisters (inciting incident). After recuperating, Jane accepts a position as teacher in the village school (rising action), and while she grieves the loss of Mr. Rochester, she makes peace with her new position—and her total loss of independence. She assumes that the dream of having a family is impossible, but maybe in time she can become financially independent by working.

However, Jane learns that Mr. Rivers and his sisters have an uncle who has just died and has cut them out of a large inheritance in favor of some mysterious other child. Yes, this is the uncle in Madeira, and the mysterious child is Jane herself (midpoint). Suddenly Jane has both independence and social position. But she has never wanted a position in society. She wants kin, family, and she now has that, too. She divides the inheritance between the four of them and makes a home out of Moor House (false victory).

It soon becomes clear that the frosty and unremittingly dour Mr. Rivers views Jane as more than a cousin. But in order to please him, Jane must compromise herself. There's no joy or vivacity around Mr. Rivers. Even when he proposes to her (tragic climax), he speaks of the marriage as more like labor than love. She will be a missionary's wife in India and live a life of duty. She will have independence but no love.

She refuses (semi-resolution).

Ferndean: The Final Resolution

There are a few gothic moments in this novel, and one comes when Jane believes she hears Mr. Rochester calling to her (inciting incident). She decides she must go to Thornfield to find out what happened to him. Upon arrival, she discovers the house burned to the ground and learns that Bertha both set the fire and died in it (rising action). In attempting to save its inhabitants, Mr. Rochester lost his eyesight and the use of one hand. He went to live in an isolated home in the woods called Ferndean with some caretakers.

Jane rushes over and is reunited with her true love (climax). Both of them are changed: Jane is now a wealthy woman in her own right, and Mr. Rochester is no longer her superior. But his love for her has endured. They come together as equals, which is significant in a society where social standing is so important. Jane gets both what she wants—independence—and what she needs—love.

Contrary to popular belief, one of the most famous last lines of literature ("Reader, I married him") is not actually the last line of the novel. But it's still pretty great. Mr. Rochester eventually regains sight in one eye and sees the birth of his first child (final resolution).

Why Is *Jane Eyre* a Classic?

Jane Eyre has stood the test of time not only because of Jane's character, which demonstrates the power of persistence and thinking for oneself, but also because of the important statement it makes about women's independence. Regardless of the hard circumstances in which Jane finds herself, she never sees herself as a victim; she pursues independence at any cost. She may not be equal to the people around her in terms of social class, but in terms of emotional maturity and intelligence, she holds her own.

The novel's dual nature as a coming-of-age and romance allows Brontë to demonstrate that independence is possible for a woman at every stage of her life, including when she marries.

Chapter Summary: Eyre Apparent

Jane Eyre is a structural mash-up that defies conventional genre boundaries. Charlotte Brontë weaves gothic romance and coming-of-age into an episodic narrative centered around distinct settings. Each location—Gateshead Hall, Lowood School, Thornfield Hall,

Moor House, and Ferndean—marks a pivotal stage in Jane's development and quest for independence. While each episode has its own arc, the resolutions are deliberately incomplete until the very end, in a way that mirrors Jane's ongoing battle against societal limitations. By intertwining these genres in this innovative structure, Brontë has crafted a novel that is both a transformative journey and a critique of Victorian society's expectations of women.

Setting as Structure: Brontë's intentional use of different settings to structure the novel allows us to think about setting as more than just background. It can also be an organizational tool, a way of delineating time periods in a protagonist's life and placing natural boundaries around various episodes or eras.

Setting brings with it many powerful immersive details that can, over time, also carry the emotional weight of memory for the protagonist—as it does for Jane. Each setting becomes a shorthand for a different period in her life, making it so much more than simply a place where something happens.

Bildungsroman Versus Coming-of-Age: All bildungsromans are coming-of-age stories, but not all coming-of-age stories are bildungsromans. A bildungsroman is a literary genre focusing on the psychological and moral growth of the protagonist from youth to adulthood. It emphasizes personal development, education, and the journey toward self-discovery and societal integration. The narrative typically spans many years, highlighting the protagonist's maturation through various experiences.

A coming-of-age story concentrates on a specific period or event in the protagonist's youth that marks their transition to maturity or self-awareness. It doesn't necessarily cover the entire journey into adulthood but more often focuses on formative moments that lead to significant personal insight.

The episodic nature of this plot structure can be very helpful when considering how to handle a novel that spans so many years. It's hard to sustain a narrative goal for a character's entire lifetime—but variations on a goal can work well. Episodic storytelling allows for arcs with semi-resolutions and a complete resolution at the end. Also, a theme common to each of the arcs can create cohesion, just as the quest for independence does in *Jane Eyre*.

The Bell Jar

by Sylvia Plath

Almost a Memoir

The Bell Jar by Sylvia Plath is an autobiographical account of the author's experience with mental illness. Though the narrative mirrors her own life, Plath opted to publish it as a novel, which allowed her to increase the drama and conceal identities. Rather than memoir, the book could be considered early autofiction (or proto-autofiction, since that term wasn't coined until 1977), along the lines of *A Portrait of the Artist as a Young Man* by James Joyce. That is to say, it's more autobiographical than a novel in which the author draws on their experiences within an otherwise invented storyline.

This is an important distinction when considering the structure of *The Bell Jar*. While memoir and autofiction rely on many of the same storytelling fundamentals as fiction, these genres allow for more structural flexibility. For example, a memoir may be built around a series of thematically connected events, and autofiction can involve a wide-ranging exploration of self (making it somewhat similar to the bildungsroman or coming-of-age novel).

Let Me Tell You About the Time That I…

As developmental editors, we get the opportunity to give feedback on a variety of memoirs-in-progress. There is one piece of advice we give to almost every client: *zoom in*. The typical memoirs we read are too sprawling, trying to encompass too much of the author's life. The power of a memoir lies in its specificity, or its "aboutness."

We often tell our memoir clients—imagine you are sitting down with an old friend you haven't seen in decades. Over an evening of catch-up conversation, you relay anecdote after anecdote, each starting with the words, "Let me tell you about the time that I..." This is the sort of specificity a memoir needs to harness. And that's exactly what Plath gives us in *The Bell Jar*.

Before we consider how that sentence might end in Plath's case, here's a quick summary of the novel:

Esther Greenwood, a talented young poet and college student, lands a prestigious internship at a fashion magazine in New York, but her excitement quickly turns to disillusionment as she grapples with the pressures of work, her relationships, a complicated dynamic with her boyfriend Buddy Willard, and societal expectations for women to marry and have children. Her descent into a mental health crisis culminates in a suicide attempt and subsequent admission to a psychiatric facility. In the institution, Esther undergoes electroconvulsive therapy and faces the daunting prospect of integrating her experiences into a semblance of normalcy as she tentatively steps toward recovery.

In other words: *Let me tell you about the time that I was hospitalized for a mental health crisis.*

Narrative Goal

While Esther Greenwood's mental health crisis has a clear focus or "aboutness," it also presents a narrative problem: it lacks a trajectory for the protagonist. That is to say, there isn't a clear *plot* inherent in someone having a breakdown and ending up hospitalized. As Esther loses her grip on reality, she becomes subject to the will of others—family and doctors. That makes her a passive protagonist who can't struggle and strive toward a clear and specific narrative goal.

Trajectory—a protagonist's effort or the rising action toward a narrative goal—is an important component of a reader's emotional draw. It allows us to connect with a protagonist through what they want, what they are willing to do (or not) to get what they want, and how they must change in order to get there. A trajectory also gives readers an idea of what the story's climax might involve.

What's fascinating about *The Bell Jar* is that Plath manages to build in a trajectory that is secondary to the main events of the novel. But make no mistake, the story is first and foremost about Esther's breakdown, hospitalization, and recovery.

It's worth noting that trajectory is not the only source of emotional draw. Plath sucks readers in with the power of her prose and the tragedy of this young woman who is robbed of her fledgling independence by her brain's revolt. However, Plath still incorporates a fully realized plotline into the novel: inciting incident, point of no return, rising action, the all-is-lost stage and subsequent helping hand, and a climax wherein her narrative goal is achieved.

So What Exactly Is Esther's Narrative Goal?

When Esther discovers that her boyfriend casually and unapologetically cheated on her, she declares that she will "go out and sleep with somebody myself." In other words, she will seize her independence—over her life, body, and boyfriend—by losing her virginity.

PLOT POINTS

Stasis

As an intelligent young woman venturing into the world, Esther Greenwood wants many things. She wants to win a scholarship to a prestigious university. She wants to build connections and experiences in the writing and editing world. She wants to write and publish her own work. What she most definitely doesn't want is to be tied down by marriage and children. In other words, she wants independence.

This is Esther's "normal life" that is about to be shattered by a disruption, upheaval, or catalyst of some kind. Her underlying motivation will be given specificity and trajectory by the inciting incident.

However, in *The Bell Jar*, Esther's stasis is not shown directly since the story opens after her inciting incident, which we'll examine next. We learn about her stasis through asides and flashbacks to a time before the bell jar has begun its descent (a metaphor for her breakdown and loss of self). This is the time before "All the little successes I'd totted up so happily at college fizzled to nothing." It's also a time when she still adored Buddy Willard, her boyfriend.

Inciting Incident

Chapter One opens sometime after Esther Greenwood's inciting incident, and even after she crosses her threshold or point of no return. We don't learn about her inciting incident until Chapter Six. In flashback, she recalls the day she visited Buddy Willard at the hospital where he was interning. In a spectacular demonstration of character, Buddy shows her a cadaver, a series of fetuses preserved in jars, a woman giving birth, and then finally, his penis. What a day.

After refusing to get naked with him, Esther asks if he's ever had sex. When he tells her about an affair that he had the summer before in Cape Cod, she is crushed and disillusioned by the betrayal. She brands Buddy as a hypocrite. He treats Esther like she's wild and lascivious, and meanwhile he was having an affair, for which he offers no apology.

This is the catalyst for her narrative goal: to get back at Buddy by losing her virginity to someone else. She wants to even the score.

It's uncertain if this is also the genesis of her depression. She comments at one point that she hasn't been happy since she was nine—ever since her father's death. So it seems depression has followed her through adolescence. But still, Buddy's betrayal has a big impact on Esther, which no doubt contributes to her looming mental health crisis.

Point of No Return

Esther's goal of getting back at Buddy and losing her virginity to someone else requires separation. And that's what she gets when Buddy is diagnosed with tuberculosis and sent away to convalesce—until Buddy's mother tries to get her a job at the sanatorium where he's staying. But then Esther, along with eleven other female college students, wins a coveted editing position with a New York fashion magazine. She accepts, taking a step toward independence.

But again, readers learn about this from asides and flashbacks.

Rising Action

When the story opens, Esther is already in New York for what is supposed to be an amazing summer of being wined and dined and presented around town. But depression is creeping in. She doesn't like most of the other students, she's bored by the parties, and the summer heat is unbearable. Her discontent with Buddy is driving her to meet someone else, but it's also getting in the way of her ability to connect with anyone.

Eventually she goes on a date with a translator named Constantin, but their encounter ends with awkwardness rather than romance. Then, at the end of her internship, she meets a man named Marco at a country club dance who tries to rape her.

Following this traumatic encounter, Esther's application to a writing program is rejected, and Buddy writes to say that he's falling in love with someone else. At this point, she is deep into her mental health crisis.

The Bell Jar was published in 1963, and much has changed in the field of psychiatry since then. As such, Esther Greenwood doesn't receive a clear diagnosis other than "depression." Some scholars contend she is dealing with bipolar II disorder. Others say it's major depressive disorder. From our own experiences with friends and loved ones with bipolar disorder, Esther's condition looks a lot like a depressive period leading into the full-blown mania of bipolar I. She goes without sleep for more than a week, even longer without bathing or changing her clothes, she can no longer read or write, and her behavior becomes erratic.

Whether due to bipolar or major depressive disorder, Esther Greenwood's breakdown reaches a peak that results in her mother's intervention.

All Is Lost

Mrs. Greenwood takes Esther to see Doctor Gordon, a psychiatrist. Esther doesn't like him and decides not to confide in him, but she does agree to come back. In a subsequent session, he gives her an electroconvulsive treatment that goes badly. Her condition worsens, and she fixates on suicide. Then, after Esther's mother takes her to visit her father's grave, she hides in the cellar and swallows a handful of sleeping pills.

Her mother finds her and gets her to the hospital. At this point, the protagonist's breakdown has eclipsed her efforts toward independence. She has become disconnected from her sense of self and lashes out at the nurses and hospital staff, which gets her sent to the psych ward. Her actions are appalling and quite disconnected from who she was—the up-and-coming young writer who won a fancy internship.

Resurgence: The Helping Hand

Following the all-is-lost moment, a protagonist may have a personal resurgence as they learn a key detail or realize something important about themselves (perhaps that what they want isn't actually what they need). However, sometimes the resurgence occurs because of an ally who arrives to help the protagonist up from rock bottom.

In Esther's case, this help comes in the form of Philomena Guinea, her benefactor. According to Wikipedia, Philomena is based on Plath's real-life benefactor, the author Olive Higgins Prouty, who funded her college studies. When she hears about Esther's suicide attempt, Philomena swoops in and gets Esther transferred into a private psychiatric hospital, where she is put under the care of Doctor Nolan, a young woman whom Esther immediately respects.

With Doctor Nolan's help and some gentler (or more capably administered) electroconvulsive treatments, Esther's bell jar begins to lift.

Climax

Whenever we're analyzing the plot of a more structurally experimental novel, we start by considering what happens at the climax. A story's climax is the answer to a question asked in the beginning, and that question comes out of the inciting incident: will the protagonist realize their narrative goal?

Now that the bell jar is lifting and Esther is feeling more like herself again, she talks to Doctor Nolan about birth control. Her breakdown was a significant barrier to many of her motivations, especially her vow to have sex with someone other than Buddy Willard.

Earlier in the story, she was hoping to meet someone nice, to start a new relationship, but now she is ready to move beyond society's contrived notions of purity and have a one-night stand. On an evening away from the hospital, Esther meets a math professor and accomplishes her goal. However, their intercourse causes her to hemorrhage, and she has to go to the hospital.

While Esther achieves her quest in the end, it does not give her the fulfillment or reprisal she sought. Shortly after this bittersweet victory, her friend commits suicide. This is Joan, a character with whom Esther has much in common. They both dated Buddy. They both excelled in school. And they were both hospitalized for attempted suicide. In fact, they have so much in common, it seems likely that Joan represents a part of Esther that has died in this ordeal and that she must leave behind.

Resolution

Esther's recovery is coming along so well, it's now time for her discharge interview. Soon she will be able to attend college and regain control of her life. Compassion and calm are returning to her, evidenced in how she deals with Buddy in this final scene—she reassures him that he had nothing to do with her breakdown or Joan's, and she reacts with indifference when he asks who might marry her now that she's been institutionalized.

She doesn't know who will marry her, but since she has been resistant to the idea of marriage all along, this is in itself a small victory—a milestone of independence. And in a final act that allows her to take back control of her sexuality, she calls the math professor and gets him to pay for her hospital bill. In response, he asks when he will see her again. "Never," she says and hangs up on him. Esther Greenwood isn't sure what will come next, and she's scared, but she's back in charge of her life.

> I took a deep breath and listened to the old brag of my heart. I am, I am, I am.

She pauses on the threshold of the interview room, collects herself, and then steps inside.

Why Is *The Bell Jar* a Classic?

Sylvia Plath committed suicide about a month after *The Bell Jar* was published. Some have speculated this was precipitated by her husband cheating on her, but clearly she was again grappling with her mental health. Had she not killed herself, we suspect any other novels she wrote would have reached a similar level of fame. Certainly her poetry is highly regarded, even the work she wrote weeks before her death.

The Bell Jar is a powerhouse of both prose and voice. Esther Greenwood comes alive on the page with her characteristic insights and metaphors. On top of this, Plath takes us deep into the experience of a mental health crisis with brutal honesty, especially at a time when the stigma around a "crack-up" was so high. This is likely why she shifted what is essentially a memoir into a novel and published it under a pseudonym.

In many of the analyses and reviews we looked at for this Skeleton, readers facing similar mental health struggles reported finding their experiences reflected and validated in this novel. Even though the field of psychiatry has changed considerably since 1963, Plath gives readers a window into her authentic experience.

However, the novel also faces contemporary scrutiny, and not for the mental health stigma it once contended with. There are several instances of racism that unfortunately diminish Esther's character. Some might say this is a sad reflection of the time Plath was living in, but there are many other novels from the '50s and '60s that are free of such language and prejudice. Others might say the racist asides and actions are a product of her mental health crisis, that Esther's breakdown robbed her of compassion. When she kicks a Black hospital worker for delivering a meal with two different kinds of beans, she is definitely disconnected from self and reality. But there is no way to know for sure, and racism in literature is more deserving of reflection and discussion of its impact than it is of apologist excuses.

Esther Greenwood's character may not sit comfortably with all readers; critique of these issues is warranted, though some may choose to skip the novel rather than bother with critique. Still, Plath was a talented writer with a powerful experience to relay—a loss of self and resurgence that so many people experience in all the forms depression and mental illness may take.

Chapter Summary: A World Under Glass

Sylvia Plath might bury her protagonist's narrative goal, but it's still there. She starts the novel after the inciting incident has already occurred and employs flashbacks and asides to fill the reader in.

When in doubt about either a protagonist's goal or the inciting incident, study the climax to determine what question is being answered. Chances are good you will then be able to pinpoint the moment when the narrative goal takes shape and the story is launched.

This is also a good way to ensure that you have chosen the right inciting incident for your own story. If there isn't a clear trajectory from inciting incident to climax, you might need to adjust one or the other to make sure they line up.

Autofiction Versus Autobiographical Fiction: Autofiction is a literary genre that blends autobiography with fiction. In autofiction, the author draws heavily from their own life experiences but intentionally incorporates fictional elements such as imagined events, altered timelines, or composite characters. The protagonist often shares the author's name or significant traits, blurring the lines between reality and invention. Autofiction allows writers to explore personal truths and subjective realities without being confined to factual accuracy, offering creative freedom to delve into deeper emotional or psychological themes.

Autobiographical fiction, on the other hand, is a genre in which the author writes a novel based on their own life but presents it as a fictional narrative. While rooted in real events and experiences, autobiographical fiction typically disguises characters and situations by changing names, locations, and details to protect privacy or enhance the storytelling. The emphasis is on crafting a coherent and engaging story that resonates with universal themes, even if it departs from strict factual truth.

The Structure of a Memoir: While memoirs are rooted in real events, they benefit from employing narrative structures commonly found in fiction to enhance engagement and emotional impact.

Consider the difference between memoir and autobiography. An autobiography is the story *of* someone's life. A memoir is a story *from* someone's life. Autobiographies are nearly impossible to sell unless the subject is famous. They simply aren't that interesting in terms of storytelling. Without a specific trajectory, they tend to lack emotional draw. The specificity of memoir creates greater immediacy and also stronger character connection, because we see who a character truly is when they're in the midst of struggling toward something they want.

Key Structural Elements of a Memoir:

- **Specific Focus (Aboutness):** A memoir should center on a specific theme, event, or period rather than attempting to cover an entire life. This focus provides clarity and depth, allowing readers to connect with the narrator's journey on a personal level.

- **Narrative Goal:** Establishing a clear objective or quest gives the memoir direction. The narrator's pursuit of this goal drives the story forward and maintains reader interest. It is also a powerful source of characterization.

- **Inciting Incident:** This is the moment that disrupts the narrator's normal life and sets them on a new path. It should be a significant event that crystallizes the narrative goal and propels the story into motion.

- **Climax and Resolution:** The memoir should build toward a climax—a pivotal moment when the central conflict reaches its peak. The resolution follows, providing closure to the narrator's journey as they reflect on the lessons learned.

Applying Fiction Techniques to Memoir Writing:

- **Use Balanced Pacing:** Keep the narrative engaging by balancing moments of tension and reflection. Avoid unnecessary tangents that don't contribute to the central theme or goal.

- **Develop Fully Realized Characters:** Including yourself! Show your characters' complexities, motivations, and growth throughout the story.

- **Create Conflict and Stakes:** Highlight the challenges and obstacles you faced in pursuing your narrative goal. Clarify what is at stake to heighten the reader's emotional investment.

- **Develop Themes:** Weave in overarching themes that offer insight into universal human experiences. This adds depth and relatability to your personal story.

- **Employ the *Show, Don't Tell* Rule*:* Engage readers by illustrating events through vivid scenes, sensory details, and dialogue. Allow readers to experience the story alongside you rather than simply recounting events.

As I Lay Dying

by William Faulkner

A Tapestry of Unreliable Narrators

William Faulkner's *As I Lay Dying* has long been hailed as a cornerstone of American literature, for both its innovative narrative style and poetic prose. The novel, set in the Deep South, tells the story of the Bundren family's journey to fulfill their matriarch Addie's dying wish to be buried in Jefferson, Mississippi. This seemingly straightforward plot serves as the backdrop for a rich ensemble of character voices and perspectives. In fact, the plot's simplicity counterbalances the complexity of perspective and unreliable narration.

The story begins with Addie Bundren's impending death and her request to be buried far from her home. As the family embarks on their journey to honor this wish, they encounter numerous obstacles, both physical and emotional. The journey is a crucible that reveals the complex inner lives of this family, especially that of the enigmatic Darl, whose perspective dominates the novel. Darl's existential musings and eventual descent into madness provide a dark counterpoint to the dysfunctional family's saga.

Much of the novel unfolds in stream-of-consciousness monologues rather than action-based scenes and dialogue. While this storytelling method could reduce the amount of direct "experience" in which the reader is immersed, Faulkner's approach allows us to examine the events of the narrative from multiple perspectives. As a result, the experience comes through in layers. Plus, Faulkner's prose is immersive in its own right. The result is a story as much about the unreliability of perception as it is about the events themselves.

Much has already been written about stream of consciousness and unreliable narration in As I Lay Dying, specifically about how the various focal characters offer conflicting accounts of each other, but there is another powerful tool in Faulkner's toolbox that often goes unexamined: how each character is defined by their individual narrative trajectories. There is the overarching trajectory—the family's journey to Jefferson—but each character also has their own narrative goal that sets them apart in the Bundren family tableau. Therein lies the power of Faulkner's characterization.

PLOT POINTS

When Addie Bundren requests to be buried in her hometown of Jefferson, her family must undertake a challenging journey to honor her wishes, with each member driven by personal motives and desires that complicate their shared mission. In fact, the story's stakes come more from the individual character goals than the family's goal. If they decided against taking Addie's body to Jefferson, their neighbors might look down upon them—though they already do. Yet they would also understand since the river crossing is treacherous at this time of year and the Bundrens have little money. Only three of them are driven to complete the mission for Addie's sake: Jewel, Cash, and (at least initially) Darl. But let's set aside the individual goals for now while we examine the main trajectory.

Stasis and Inciting Incident

The story begins after the inciting incident has taken place. Addie Bundren is dying, and she has made her final wishes known: she wants to be buried in Jefferson. This establishes a narrative goal for the rest of the family: once she dies, they must honor her wishes.

But the goal is actually more complex than that. In honoring her wishes, they must come to terms with her death, each in their own way. For this reason, the pronouncement of her final wish is the inciting incident, not her death. Each family member will approach this quest differently, and that quest begins *as she lays dying*.

The stasis, for the family and for each individual, is the status quo before the disruption. This is something we learn about as the story unfolds, in part from Addie's intuitive son Darl, but also from Addie herself. The novel isn't always linear; it's not until a later chapter that we get some cold hard truth about Mom and her relationship with the rest of them. Motherhood wasn't what she'd hoped for. She resented her husband Anse. She cheated on him with a local holy man and thereby had her son Jewel. And then she bore Anse two more children out of a sense of duty but not love. Of all the children, Jewel is the one she loved most, in part because he was born of her defiance of a social order which she held in contempt.

Initial Rising Action

In many narratives, the rising action begins after the point of no return. However, in *As I Lay Dying*, the family must wait for Addie to die before they can set out on their journey, so the Bundrens begin their emotional journey before the physical one.

The father, Anse, is self-serving. Even before Addie dies, he demonstrates his lack of empathy by sending his sons (Darl and Jewel) on a delivery job that will net them a whopping three dollars and quite probably deny them the chance to be present for their mother's final moments. Darl is Anse's foil: he cares deeply for his family, and though he begrudgingly agrees to the delivery, he agonizes over his absence at his mother's deathbed. Meanwhile, the eldest son, Cash, demonstrates his commitment to hard work and duty by building his mother's coffin. Jewel, the third son, is angry that Cash is building a coffin in Addie's sight, demonstrating both his fierce loyalty to his mother and his unwillingness to accept her coming death. Dewey Dell, the only girl, eagerly anticipates her mother's death, since the trip to Jefferson is an opportunity for her to get an abortion. And Vardaman, the youngest (his age isn't revealed, but he's probably five or six), struggles to make sense of the entire scenario.

Point of No Return

This plot point arrives with Addie's death. The family is now committed to fulfilling her final wish.

Rising Action Continues

As they prepare to depart, interpersonal conflict reveals more about the characters:

- Cash insists on bringing his carpentry tools, and he's frustrated that the coffin hasn't been properly balanced on the wagon. This is another demonstration of his commitment to duty and hard work.

- Jewel doesn't want to ride on the wagon with the others; he insists on riding his own horse. This reinforces his pride and his separation from the others. (We never get Jewel's perspective; his character is revealed only through his coldness and occasional surges of emotion. Thus, the reader is as alienated from him as his family is.)

- Even though Jewel rides off in anger, Darl declares that Jewel will follow them once he has had a chance to cool off, which he does. This is a clue to Darl's role as the heart of the family: he sees their truths and negotiates for their unity.

- When Jewel does return, he storms past them on his horse, which throws up mud that lands on the coffin. In response, Cash wipes off the mud and tries to clean the stain. Again, we see Jewel's single-minded determination to escort his mother to Jefferson while maintaining distance from the others. Cash's focus on duty, his role as carpenter, and the coffin itself are all embodiments of his dedication.

- When they arrive at a washed-out bridge, they must decide how to proceed. Anse, while bemoaning his fate as a poor, hardworking farmer, stands around indecisively while his sons are forced to come up with a plan. As with the earlier conflict when he sends Darl and Jewel on an ill-timed delivery run for little money, Anse demonstrates that he is weak and ineffectual.

Midpoint

The river crossing goes badly. Both mules drown. The family nearly loses the coffin and Cash's tools, and Cash breaks his leg. This incident significantly complicates their path forward. They no longer have a team to pull the wagon, and they don't have enough money for Cash to visit a doctor. It is also around this point when Darl intuits that Jewel has a different father.

Rising Action Continues

In his first true causal action of the story, Anse rejects an offer to borrow some horses and instead trades Jewel's horse for a new team to pull the wagon. Jewel is infuriated. He worked hard to buy his steed, and again it seems like he will run off, but he doesn't. He remains committed to the journey for his mother's sake.

Cash's leg causes him tremendous pain, so they come up with the terrible idea of securing the break with cement.

Dewey Dell visits a pharmacist and asks about medicine for an abortion, but she's turned away.

All Is Lost (and Yet More Rising Action)

Darl is struggling. His mental health is declining. In part this is because of his earlier realization that Jewel was the product of their mother's adultery, and at this point he lets Jewel know, which goes about as well as you might expect. Darl is also struggling because his mother's body is in a horrific state of decay; the stench is all around them. He sees this as an affront to her dignity, or perhaps more to the family's dignity. He is, after all, the empath in their midst. He decides to take matters into his own hands and sets fire to the barn that houses the coffin in the hope that the fire will consume Addie's corpse, thereby ending their miserable journey.

This is the all-is-lost moment in terms of the family's overarching quest, since it's the point in the story when they are brought closest to failure. However, it's admittedly an atypical all-is-lost moment since Darl, as the principal POV character, drives the action. For Darl, the barn burning is more of a tragic climax—tragic because he doesn't succeed. Jewel runs into the burning barn and, in a heroic feat of strength and obsessive desperation, rescues the coffin. Darl's failure to burn Addie's body also represents a failure to restore the family's equilibrium. That's because Vardaman witnesses Darl's arson and tells Dewey Dell, and then someone (presumably Dewey Dell) tells the barn owner that her brother was responsible.

Following the barn incident, Darl makes one last attempt to pull the family together. He intervenes when Jewel almost gets himself stabbed, and he insists on a doctor for Cash as his brother's foot is turning black. However, someone must answer for the arson, and Darl's grip on reality is deteriorating, so the family conspires to have him committed.

Resurgence and Climax

In having Darl committed, the family is able to rebound from the all-is-lost moment. Darl is fingered for the arson and is punished accordingly. This betrayal also removes a destabilizing force, at least from the perspectives of Jewel, Dewey Dell, and Anse. Of course, from Darl's perspective, he was trying his best to be a force for equilibrium. This is a great example of how divergent their perspectives really are.

Jewel is furious about Darl's suggestion that he has a different father than the other siblings. Whether he knows it's true is another question. It could be that Addie told him, but it could also be that she merely favored him, which set him apart from his siblings. She named him Jewel, after all. He has also, presumably, written off his brother for attempting to burn their mother's corpse.

Dewey Dell's issue with Darl is that he can see through her—he knew immediately that she was pregnant, even though she hadn't told anyone. Like Jewel, she seeks to be separate from the rest of the family. Darl threatens that isolation with his insights; he sees what she would keep hidden.

Ultimately, Jewel and Dewey Dell are both happy to see Darl locked up. As for Anse, Darl is a convenient sacrifice that sorts out the trouble with the destroyed barn. Cash's betrayal in supporting Darl's hospitalization comes with the most sting. He doesn't have an issue with Darl, but since he is all about duty, he supports the status quo.

With Darl out of the way, Anse borrows some shovels (presumably from an old acquaintance), and finally they bury Addie in Jefferson as she requested. The quest is fulfilled, at least for Jewel and Cash. Jewel was bound by honor to see Addie to her final rest, while Cash was bound by duty.

Resolution

Two more quests are wrapped up after Addie is in the ground. First, Dewey tries again to obtain medicine for an abortion, but she is tricked and sexually assaulted by the pharmacist's assistant. Hers is a tragic resolution: she betrayed her brother so she could keep her secret, but now nothing will hide the truth growing in her womb.

Afterward, Anse takes the ten dollars she saved for her abortion. With this money, he heads into town and achieves what he really wanted out of this trip to Jefferson. He wasn't all that concerned with laying Addie to rest. Right from the start, he had his sights on a set of dentures and a replacement wife. With Dewey Dell's money in hand, he buys himself a set of teeth. When he returns, he also has a new wife with him. Apparently, the person he borrowed the shovels from was more than a mere acquaintance.

Each Character Has a Different Goal

The Bundren family is on a quest to bury Addie in Jefferson, but they each have different reasons for doing so, or at least different approaches to the journey. The voyage gives the story a through-line plot, while the character goals add narrative depth at the level of characterization and theme.

Anse

As mentioned above, Anse's main motivation for the trip is to buy a set of dentures and find a new wife. He also wants to maintain appearances with the neighbors by burying Addie and fulfilling her dying wish, but it's not for love or duty. The journey is more of a convenience to achieve his actual goal. Anse is self-serving and opportunistic. He's also lazy, and therein lie the stakes for his personal quest: he needs a wife to manage the household for him.

Jewel and Cash

Both brothers are committed to their mother's dying wish, Jewel because he takes pride in the fact that Addie loved him above the rest and Cash because he is devoted to duty and the status quo. The stakes for them are deeply personal. Succeeding in their quest means holding true to who they are. If they fail Addie, they will have failed themselves.

Dewey Dell

The sister has three significant moments of causal action that relate to her goal of obtaining an abortion: her two pharmacy visits and her act of betraying Darl. Ultimately, she wants her secret kept. She doesn't seem to care much that her mother is dying. In the beginning, she wishes it along, if only to arrive in Jefferson sooner, which is where she hopes to petition a pharmacist for help.

Vardaman

The youngest sibling is in a constant state of trying to understand what is happening—from his mother's death to the nature of being (something he discusses in perplexing terms with Darl) to Darl's eventual descent into madness.

Darl

Up until the final section, Darl is the primary narrator. He is at once intuitive, intelligent, and confused as he tries his best to make sense of the world and of his family members. His goal is to hold the family together emotionally. Thematically, Darl represents the family's emotional core. He sees the truth in each of them, which makes him the most caring and compassionate of the characters, but in the end his insights lead to his mental breakdown.

The rest of the Bundren family is on this quest for self-serving reasons. The irony is that they are all isolated from each other by these selfish pursuits, even in Cash's desire to prove his dutifulness, such that he is willing to betray his brother—duty for duty's sake. And aside from Cash, we've got Jewel, who is the embodiment of his mother's pride; Anse, who is a self-serving fool; Dewey Dell, who is the self-isolated betrayer; and Vardaman, who is too young to understand and perhaps too impressionable to escape the dysfunction that surrounds him. Thus, Darl's goal is a hopeless one.

In the end, seeing the truth about his family is his undoing. They are too full of contradiction and hypocrisy to be redeemable, so he is more alone than any of them. This is not just the culmination of Darl's arc, but also the revelation of Faulkner's chosen narrative style: we see these characters' failings through his eyes, but also through the unreliable narration of each of them and the people they meet along the way.

What's in a Name?

As I Lay Dying is a novel rich with hidden meanings and subtle symbolism. While the story was written in the stream-of-consciousness tradition of Joyce and Woolf, it is far from a random or unstructured narrative. Faulkner imbues his characters and their surroundings with significant clues that illuminate the deeper themes of the novel. One of the most compelling examples of this is the symbolism found in the characters' names.

- **Bundren**, the family name, is more or less a reconfiguration of burden.
- **Addie**, or Adelaide, means "a noble kind," and she certainly demands a sort of nobility in her request to be buried far from home.

- **Jewel** is, of course, Addie's jewel. He represents all that is precious to her—her defining act of independence in what she otherwise saw as a life of subordination.
- **Cash** also means value, but it's the everyday value of hard work, as opposed to a precious stone that contains value in and of itself.
- **Anse**, some have argued, might be a reference to *anserous*, which means goose-like or stupid.
- **Vardaman** might refer to verdant, as in green or growing, or it might be a play on vard/ward, which is Scottish for an underage orphan.
- **Dewey** suggests morning dew, which could refer to her innocence and fertility, and **Dell** suggests a small, secluded valley, symbolic of her isolation and the secret she seeks to keep hidden.
- **Darl** is short for darling. He is the honest heart within a rotting whole.

Why Is *As I Lay Dying* a Classic?

There's a lot going on in this novel. Especially impressive is that Faulkner wrote *As I Lay Dying* in six weeks, with no revisions—by hand and, apparently, on onionskin paper. This novel, among the others he wrote, netted him the Nobel Prize for Literature. So, clearly, there are some brains behind the page. There is also a tremendous amount of poetry in the prose, especially in Darl's monologues and his conversations with Vardaman.

That being said, this book isn't an easy read. The current Goodreads rating is 3.7/5. Many readers love the novel to pieces, but others are frustrated by what they describe as needless obfuscation. Faulkner doesn't make clarity a priority, especially with so many contrary perspectives and a nonlinear presentation. Still, for those who take the time to immerse themselves in the unusual voice and style, there is a lot to appreciate here:

> In a strange room you must empty yourself for sleep. And before you are emptied for sleep, what are you. And when you are emptied for sleep, you are not. And when you are filled with sleep, you never were. I don't know what I am. I don't know if I am or not. Jewel knows he is, because he does not know that he does not know whether he is or not. He cannot empty himself for sleep because he is not what he is and he is what he is not. Beyond the unlamped wall I can hear the rain shaping the wagon that is ours, the load that is no longer theirs that felled and sawed it nor yet theirs that bought it and which is not ours either, lie on our wagon though it does, since only the wind and the rain shape it only to Jewel and me, that are not asleep. And since sleep is is-not and rain and wind are *was*, it is not. Yet the wagon *is*, because when the wagon is *was*, Addie Bundren will not be. And Jewel *is*, so Addie Bundren must be. And then I must be, or I could not empty myself for sleep in a strange room.

Chapter Summary: Worst Road Trip Ever

As I Lay Dying is a fantastic case study of multilayered structure and unreliable narration, with each character's journey providing a different thematic angle on the Bundren family's quest to bury Addie. The novel's intricate use of language and symbolism challenges readers to consider the complexity of perception and reality. Faulkner's innovative approach to storytelling not only deepens our understanding of the characters but also underscores the novel's exploration of isolation, empathy, selfishness, and the human condition.

Stream of Consciousness: Stream of consciousness is a narrative technique that aims to depict the continuous flow of a character's thoughts, feelings, and sensory experiences as they occur in real time. Originating in the early twentieth century, it became a hallmark of modernist literature, with authors like James Joyce, Virginia Woolf, and Marcel Proust pioneering its use. This style attempts to mirror the natural, often nonlinear way the human mind works, capturing the chaotic and associative nature of thought processes without the constraints of traditional scene-based writing.

Stream-of-consciousness narration offers readers an intimate glimpse into a character's inner world. In bypassing conventional grammar and syntax, it conveys the immediacy and spontaneity of thoughts and emotions, creating a more authentic and immersive experience. However, this approach can also pose challenges. Its fragmented and nonlinear nature may lead to confusion, making it difficult for readers to follow the plot or understand character motivations. Excessive ambiguity or a lack of clear narrative markers can obscure the story's message, potentially alienating those who prefer more structured storytelling.

Unreliable Narration: Unreliable narration is a literary device in which the credibility of the narrator is compromised, prompting readers to question the accuracy of the account being presented. This unreliability can stem from various sources: the narrator might be biased, lack critical information, suffer from psychological instability, or intentionally deceive the audience. By employing an unreliable narrator, authors invite readers to engage more actively with the text and uncover the underlying truth. However, unreliable narration can also be a double-edged sword. If not handled carefully, it may lead to confusion or frustration, potentially disengaging readers who feel manipulated or left in the dark.

Using Symbols: Symbolism can be an effective way of underscoring a novel's theme. You can use names, setting, and imagery to accomplish this goal. An image that changes over the course of the novel can be particularly effective in transmitting meaning. Readers think in symbols, whether we realize it or not. And authors often bury symbols in their work without even knowing it.

The key here is subtlety. Reading is a process of discovery. Avoid heavy-handedness and allow your readers to figure things out. Quite often, it will be enough that we notice the symbols exist.

To the Lighthouse
by Virginia Woolf

"A Novel Light on Plot"

As we scrolled through summaries of must-read classics, we stumbled upon *To the Lighthouse*, which was summarized as "a novel light on plot." That was when we knew we'd found an excellent candidate for a Story Skeleton. *To the Lighthouse* is Virginia Woolf's take on the modernist novel, the plot of which, according to Wikipedia, "is secondary to its philosophical introspection."

Much has been written about the novel's English-lit checklist of themes: love, loss, the nature of change, the war between idealism and rationalism, and the impossibility of objective truth. But less has been said about the plot, almost as if the narrative structure doesn't matter—as if the structure has little bearing on the true greatness of this work: its philosophical underpinnings, POV rollercoaster, and commentary about human nature.

In fact, there is a plot here, though it is hidden below the surface and even disguised by a narrative technique that could be called "multiple focalization" if you want to get fancy, or if not, a workshop in head hopping. More importantly, the plot is directly relevant to Woolf's philosophical and thematic explorations.

The story can be summed up as follows: Mr. and Mrs. Ramsay argue about the feasibility of a trip to visit the nearby lighthouse. Then a decade passes, during which Mrs. Ramsay dies. Then Mr. Ramsay sails to the lighthouse with two of his children.

Light on plot? Yes, indeed. To be sure, there are other things going on, but the narrative is built around these two movements: debating a trip to the lighthouse and undertaking a trip to the lighthouse. The novel draws its complexity from the roiling thoughts of the Ramsay family and all the guests staying at their summer house in Scotland. In fact, there is little in the way of action or dialogue. For the most part, readers are locked into the various characters' interiority: what they are longing for, what impassions them, what they hate or fear—and of course, what they think about each other.

But does this count as plot? Doesn't plot require a protagonist? Doesn't it require an inciting incident, an arc, and a climax?

Absolutely. But we contend that these plot elements are present in *To the Lighthouse*. To uncover them, we must first determine who the protagonist actually is.

So Who the Heck Is the Protagonist?

At the start of the book, it's easy to assume that Mrs. Ramsay is the protagonist. She is the driving force of the conflict, railing against her husband's pessimism about the weather forecast and longing to fulfill her son James' wish to go to the lighthouse. Her passion and astute observations are endearing. But then—plot twist—she dies at the midpoint. And her death is relegated to summary.

Could she be the protagonist of the first half of the novel? She does start out with the narrative goal of seeing young James' wish come true, but she doesn't have a clear arc. So no, let's set her candidacy aside.

Another possibility is Lily, a painter friend of the Ramsays. Unlike Mrs. Ramsay, Lily is there at the beginning and the end. She also has a quest of sorts, which is to complete a portrait of Mrs. Ramsay and James. Many of the story's discussions about subjectivity and the nature of art would be mute without Lily's contribution. But is this a story framed by the painting of a portrait? No, everything hinges on the lighthouse. And does Lily have the most significant arc? She offers engaging introspection, and some have suggested she is a stand-in for the author, but Lily does not undergo a fundamental change in either worldview or perspective.

The character with the most significant arc is Mr. Ramsay. At the beginning of the story, he stands up against Mrs. Ramsay's idealism as an unwavering rationalist. He is also desperate for his wife's understanding and encouragement. Mr. Ramsay is plagued by self-doubt and needs constant reassurance. And then his wife dies, leaving him to face the brutal pessimism at the heart of his so-called rationalism. While she was alive and willing to coddle him, Mr. Ramsay could use his rationalism as both a shield and an excuse, but confronted with her absence, he is forced to accept how important her idealism was to his well-being. He is forced to concede that rationalism alone is insufficient.

But Mr. Ramsay does not jump off the page as a protagonist, especially since we are inundated with the perspectives of so many other characters. Much of what we learn about him is from the outside, through the eyes and minds of others.

With Mr. Ramsay now in focus, let's look at how the plot showcases his transformation.

PLOT POINTS

Stasis

We don't get much in the way of stasis since the novel opens with the inciting incident, which we'll get to in a moment. That's not unusual—many books skip stasis or even start after the inciting incident has already occurred. Still, the stasis is implied.

As the story unfolds, we learn that Mr. Ramsay is obsessed with his legacy. He is published in the field of philosophy, but he worries that his contribution may not be significant enough for anyone to remember him forty years down the road. Within this worry, we glimpse his greater dilemma: he prides himself on his rationalism, which is actually a front for pessimism and negativity. In other words, Mr. Ramsay's underlying motivation is to deny that his negativity is anything other than a flexing of his rational powers. This allows him to feign self-assuredness, but beneath the philosopher's facade, he is very much like his son James—eager for Mrs. Ramsay's love and reassurance.

Inciting Incident

When young James says he wants to visit the lighthouse, Mrs. Ramsay is filled with her character-defining desire to give him what he wants. In fact, she fears that if James encounters a significant disappointment, it could become a memory that will haunt him (and shape him) into adulthood. The subtext here, perhaps, is that he may turn out embittered like his father.

Therefore, Mrs. Ramsay promises that they will organize a trip to the lighthouse at the earliest opportunity. This assertion strikes Mr. Ramsay as irrational. It is yet another example of his wife's idealism, which he sets in opposition to rationality. The weather is bad, and all signs point to continued wind and rain. Thus, his narrative goal is formed: he will convince his wife that her promise to James is empty, that a trip to the lighthouse will not come to pass.

Rising Action

Tensions rise between husband and wife as they squabble over meteorological predictions. Young James even considers stabbing his father. The conflict spills over into more tension with the other guests. In the end, Mr. Ramsay is correct in his assessment. The storm doesn't let up. But even so, he is not vindicated. Instead, in the eyes of everyone present, he has made an ass of himself. He has demonstrated how badly he needs to be right and how he needs to be propped up by the reassurances of his wife.

Midpoint Reversal

The summer vacation ends, after which the family does not return to Scotland for a decade. This section of the novel takes the form of detached summary. The First World War comes and goes. Mrs. Ramsay passes away, and two of Mr. Ramsay's children die.

A novel's midpoint can be many things. Sometimes it's a new opportunity for the protagonist, who has otherwise become stuck in their quest (like Dorothea in George Eliot's *Middlemarch*). Sometimes it's a shift in character focus (like in Brontë's *Wuthering Heights*). Sometimes it's a complete reversal that forces the protagonist to reassess their path forward, taking the story in an unexpected direction (like Michael in Mario Puzo's *The Godfather*).

Mr. Ramsay can no longer pursue his goal of pitting his rationalism against his wife's idealism. He no longer has her assurances to prop him up, which forces him to contend with his negativity on his own. If he gives in to it, he will remain alone and isolated. Thus, his narrative goal has changed. What he had counted on as a strength of his character has become a flaw. He can no longer reject Mrs. Ramsay's idealism; instead, he must embrace it.

Much of this happens "off camera" during the decade that is relegated to summary. But we can see evidence of this internal struggle based on what comes next.

The Beginning of Mr. Ramsay's Transformation

Also buried in summary is Mr. Ramsay's all-is-lost moment. But he clearly reaches a point in his grief and isolation where he is forced to see what he has truly lost in his wife's passing: her positivity, her desire to bring people together, to make people happy. Thus, when he consents to a reunion vacation at the summer house in Scotland after so many years, he crosses a threshold. He is softening into Mrs. Ramsay's role and embracing the positivity and idealism that he shunned for so long as antithetical to his rationalism.

But once at the summer house, Mr. Ramsay demonstrates that he is still mid-transformation. He turns to the artist Lily for the emotional support he used to get from his wife. She pities him for his fragility, and also for how his two surviving children treat him so coldly.

But then Mr. Ramsay proposes they sail to the lighthouse. James is no longer willing, and neither is his sister Cam. They wish for the wind to die down so that the passage becomes impossible. But they accompany their father all the same. At this point, the narration focuses on the interiority of Lily, Cam, and James—all three of them considering Mr. Ramsay's character, how lonely he is and how controlling. Lily also thinks a lot about Mrs. Ramsay in contrast, how much she misses her friend. But as the sailboat nears the lighthouse, all three shift in their assessment.

The first softening comes when Mr. Ramsay tells Cam not to throw her unwanted sandwich overboard—not to be wasteful. Both siblings have spent most of the trip dreading their father's "tyranny," and even though he is telling Cam what to do in this moment, "he said it so wisely," and then he gives her a gingerbread nut "as if he were a great Spanish gentleman."

Next, one of the sailors on board points out where a boat went down and three men died. Both siblings dread their father's response, that he might say something dismissive or pretentious, but he simply says, "Ah."

Keep in mind, we're dealing in subtlety here! "Ah" isn't much of a comment, but the point is, Mr. Ramsay is bucking their expectations. Even Lily back on shore notes, as if from her artistic intuition, that "Mr. Ramsay changed as he sailed further and further across the bay."

Next, Mr. Ramsay, always one to criticize, pulls out his watch and notes the quick time they've made, and he praises his son for steering them "like a born sailor." While James gives no outward reaction, Cam can guess the impact this praise has had on her brother. Here is the rebirth of Mrs. Ramsay's reassurance, passing from father to son.

Climax

When they reach the lighthouse, the protagonist's transformation is complete. Both of his children have seen him in a new light, and Lily too senses the change from shore. Again, more artistic intuition.

> "He must have reached it," said Lily Briscoe aloud, feeling suddenly completely tired out. For the Lighthouse had become almost invisible, had melted away into a blue haze, and the effort of looking at it and the effort of thinking of him landing there, which both seemed to be one and the same effort, had stretched her body and mind to the utmost. Ah, but she was relieved. Whatever she had wanted to give him, when he left her that morning, she had given him at last.

This is where the story ends—with Lily reflecting on the lighthouse trip as well as on her portrait of Mrs. Ramsay and James. In contrast to Mr. Ramsay's earlier anxiety about his legacy, she considers that the painting is likely to be hung in an attic or destroyed, but it doesn't matter. She has remained true to her vision. This is also the lesson contained within Mr. Ramsay's transformation: he has opened up; he has softened; he has eased off his need for control. His legacy as a philosopher may still be in doubt, but he has taken new steps toward posterity in his relationship with his children. Here is a legacy that will live on regardless of his intellect.

Point of View

Editors (ourselves included) frequently caution writers away from "head hopping," which is when the POV jumps from one character to the next within the same scene—even the same paragraph or sentence. Some famous authors still get away with it, but in general, it's a technique that many readers find sloppy and distracting.

But anything can be done well, especially when it's done with intentionality. In *To the Lighthouse*, Woolf is quite purposeful in this choice. The novel is a work of literary modernism, which was a movement characterized by experimental form, stream-of-consciousness prose, and epistemological themes. By jumping from one character's brain to the next, Woolf is able to explore topics such as subjectivity and perception. We learn just as much about each character through the eyes of others as from their own thoughts. This is especially true toward the end, as Mr. Ramsay's transformation is reflected in the subtle changes in perspective of Cam, James, and Lily.

Also, the shifting POV evokes the lighthouse as it shines a rotating beam into the minds of the Ramsays and their gathered friends. Some scholars have suggested the Ramsay summer home might be the narrator. Again, this is because the narrative offers no direct or experiential knowledge of the characters who aren't present. But if the narrator is the house, then the final sailing trip would fall outside that scope. It seems more likely that the lighthouse is the narrator.

Leaving the narrator's identity aside, the head-hopping narration allows for comprehensive insight into each of these characters, from within and without. In other words, Woolf's POV choice serves the story (as it always should).

Why Is *To the Lighthouse* a Classic?

Some readers struggle to get into this novel. The POV shifts can be disorienting. The dearth of plot and stakes can impact engagement. But Woolf's prose is masterful, and every character is painted with both depth and nuance. On top of that, the narrative poses nonstop questions about human perception, awareness, and the nature of knowledge and knowing.

Sigmund Freud's theories had a strong influence on modernist writers, and much of that is on display here. Mrs. Ramsay and Lily both demonstrate keen insight into the impacts of their unconscious minds, whereas the other characters are less self-aware—Mr. Ramsay least of all. Plus, the way James adores his mother and hates his father gives off undeniable Oedipal vibes.

The result is an exploration of gendered psychology, gender norms, logical positivism, and the nature of art. Mr. Ramsay is a needy tyrant who hides behind his intellect while failing to see the strength of his wife's positivity and idealism. Mrs. Ramsay is a devoted caregiver who takes her caregiving to its own tyrannical extreme by trying to engineer relationships (she is famous for playing matchmaker). And Lily is caught between her artistic vision and how others might perceive her work, just as she is at odds with her desire to remain unmarried and her society's expectations for women to find a partner.

But at the novel's core is a singular theme that connects the story structure with all these philosophical questions. In his stasis, Mr. Ramsay holds the misbelief that rationality represents the pinnacle of human cognition, and that legacy is achieved through the power of intellect. Over the course of his journey, he realizes the significance of his wife's emotional intelligence. Therefore, his subverted misbelief gives us the central theme: neither rationalism nor idealism is superior; they are two parts of a greater whole. And through that whole lies authentic connection—something greater than legacy.

Through Woolf's pioneering narrative techniques, notably the deft interplay of nuanced perspectives, *To the Lighthouse* challenges us to confront our own perceptions and biases. It compels us to engage with the text—and, by extension, with the world around us—on a new level. This is the hallmark of truly great literature: it does not merely tell a story; it invites us into a dialogue, prompting introspection and offering insights that transcend the confines of its pages.

Chapter Summary: Beam Dreams

Even though the plot in this novel may be light, it still exists, and it plays an integral role in showcasing the transformation of character. Sometimes we have to dig deeper to find things like the structure and the protagonist, but the digging pays dividends in the end, showing us just how malleable structure is and how creative we can get with it.

What's key to note here is that every one of Woolf's decisions is intentional, including her choice of POV and what she shows (versus what is implied). She uses a significant midpoint reversal to effect transformation in her protagonist and uses theme to build a bridge between structure and philosophy.

Head Hopping Versus Omniscient Narration Versus Multi-POV: To understand the distinctions between head hopping, omniscient narration, and multi-POV, it's essential to first define "deep" third-person narration (sometimes referred to as "close" third).

Deep third, the most common POV choice in modern literature, is essentially first person with the pronouns swapped. In deep third, the narrative voice belongs entirely to the focal character. Their thoughts, perceptions, and emotions filter everything on the page. The result is an intimate perspective in which the character's lived experience and internal voice shape the storytelling.

Omniscient narration, by contrast, is a voice and perspective external to the characters. An omniscient narrator is a distinct, all-seeing storyteller. They may delve into the characters' minds, revealing thoughts, feelings, and sensory impressions, but their voice remains their own. This externality makes omniscient narration less personal than deep third and more flexible for presenting multiple characters' experiences without adopting their voices (and therein lies an important but subtle difference).

In contemporary fiction, the line between omniscient narration and deep third often blurs. Head hopping is when these two POV styles get mixed together. Rather than an omniscient narrator reaching into various characters' minds, head hopping involves shifts from one deep third-person perspective to another—without warning and in the middle of a scene. While some authors get away with head hopping, it will invariably annoy many readers. That's why most editors advise authors to avoid it.

There is one more option to consider. In a multi-POV novel, the story alternates between two or more characters' deep third-person perspectives, but these shifts are clearly marked, often with chapter or section breaks. Each POV character gets their own space to fully inhabit the narrative, allowing readers to immerse themselves in one perspective at a time. Typically, multi-POV stories also ensure that each character has a distinct arc, with their own stakes, goals, and development contributing to the larger narrative.

Choosing a Narrator: While it might seem easier to jump around from one character's head to another, many readers find it distracting. When considering who should tell your story, take a look at the character who has the most significant arc. Usually, this is also the character who has the most to lose if they don't achieve their narrative goal.

Animal Farm

by George Orwell

The Structure of a Parable

Dictionary.com offers the following definition of *parable*: "A short allegorical story designed to illustrate or teach some truth, religious principle, or moral lesson."

While George Orwell's *Animal Farm*, at 140 pages, is long enough to be considered a novel, it is relatively short. But regardless of the length, it approaches narrative in the manner of a parable. As per Wikipedia, it can also be considered a satirical allegorical novella. According to Orwell, the story is meant to represent the Russian Revolution of 1917 and the establishment of the Soviet Union under Stalin.

Much has already been said about the allegory, but the narrative structure deserves a closer look. The surprising achievement of *Animal Farm* is its unusual Skeleton. Orwell has skillfully subverted traditional narrative structure while still spinning an engaging tale.

For starters, there is no true protagonist. Instead, in a nice echo of communism, the story follows the successes and failures of the farm as a whole. And yet, aside from Napoleon the antagonist, very few of the farm animals can be described as active. They aren't struggling and striving toward a goal. Instead, they are following orders, occasionally raising questions and concerns, but largely going along with the rule imposed on them by the pigs. Much of the tension, then, comes from dramatic irony—readers know what's really going on. The unfortunate animals are, for the most part, too daft to recognize the wool that's been pulled over their eyes.

If we try to frame the farm animals' plight in a logline, it doesn't quite work:

When Napoleon and the pigs take over their farm, the other animals must resist the new paradigm of oppression, otherwise they will be just as badly off as they were before the revolution.

The problem is—the animals have no recourse to resist. The pigs are smarter than they are; they can read and write, and more importantly, they are capable of deception.

So does that mean *Animal Farm* doesn't have a plot? Not at all. It's a simple one, but it's still there. The plot causality belongs almost entirely to the antagonist, Napoleon.

Narrative Goal

Napoleon drives the story from beginning to end. His goal is to wrest control of the farm from the humans and, ultimately, to become human himself. When we consider a logline from the antagonist's perspective, suddenly it works:

When the animals of Manor Farm stage a revolution and depose Mr. Jones, Napoleon maneuvers to secure himself as the supreme commander before his reign can be challenged, whether by the animals he governs or the other humans around Willingdon.

PLOT POINTS

Stasis

The animals, as governed by Mr. Jones, live a difficult life in which they must labor endlessly, are kept hungry, and are often slaughtered and sold to other humans.

Inciting Incident

A venerable boar named Old Major (feasibly Marx or Lenin) decries the animals' treatment under the human regime. He teaches the animals of Manor Farm a revolutionary song called "Beasts of England," but then he dies before he can lead the revolution. Two younger pigs, Napolean and Snowball, assume control of the animals, stage a revolt, and thus Animal Farm begins its hopeful collectivism under a new name.

Point of No Return

One could argue that the inciting incident and point of no return are one and the same. Once the animals overthrow Jones, Napoleon's gambit to install himself as supreme commander is underway. However, symbolically, the point of no return could also be the animals' adoption of the Seven Commandments of Animalism, which are painted on the barn.

Rising Action

One of the first causally crucial things Napoleon does is sequester a litter of puppies with the purpose of teaching them the principles of Animalism. In fact, he is planning ahead.

In the first major challenge to Napoleon's plans, Mr. Jones returns with other humans to take back his property. However, Napoleon and Snowball organize an effective defense, with Snowball in particular playing a heroic part and getting shot in the leg.

After the Battle of the Cowshed, Snowball proposes the animals build a windmill, which will eventually reduce their collective labor. Seeing the threat to his leadership, Napoleon declares Snowball an enemy of Animal Farm, then sends his puppies (now grown into vicious dogs) to chase Snowball away.

Following this, Napoleon convinces the animals that the windmill was his idea, and after a purge of other animals whom he claims are Snowball's spies, few are left willing to question his authority.

The first windmill fails, but with time they rebuild. Animal Farm is poised to do well.

Midpoint

Mr. Frederick, the neighboring farmer, leads a second attack and blows up the new windmill. The animals manage to repel the humans, but many are wounded, including Boxer the draft horse.

All Is Lost

The attack by Mr. Frederick leads to a new crisis for Napoleon: Benjamin the donkey figures out that Boxer has been sold to the glue factory. Boxer is well respected, and for a moment it seems the animals will finally realize the truth about Napoleon's scheme. However, the pigs spin more lies and convince the animals that Boxer has been sent to a veterinarian.

Climax

The erosion of the Seven Commandments of Animalism begins soon after Snowball is ejected, but there is still a bit more rising action for Napoleon as he makes further changes. "No animal shall kill another animal" becomes "No animal shall kill another animal… without cause." Bit by bit, he paves the way for the pigs to act more and more like humans, for example, by sleeping in beds ("No animal shall sleep in a bed" becomes "No animal shall sleep in a bed… with sheets") and drinking whiskey ("No animal shall drink alcohol" becomes "No animal shall drink alcohol… to excess").

When the pigs start wearing clothing and walking on two legs, the first commandment is changed from "Whatever goes upon two legs is an enemy" to "Two legs are better than four."

The climax comes, not in the sense of a final high-stakes drama, but in Napoleon's crowning achievement: he cements his ownership in the eyes of his human neighbors. In order to prevent humans from staging another attack, Napoleon decides to form an alliance, so he hosts a dinner party. He also ditches the revolutionary traditions that led to the formation of Animal Farm and reverts to the name Manor Farm.

Resolution

As the humans and pigs share food and whiskey and play cards together, some of the animals peer inside the farmhouse. They can no longer tell the difference between the humans and pigs.

Arc

Though there isn't a singular protagonist with a complex character arc, the farm and its inhabitants undergo substantial metamorphosis.

Initially driven by a common goal, the animals unite against human oppression. However, as the story unfolds, their unity fractures. The animals' faith in the commandments wavers, their memories of the rebellion blur, and their allegiance to the pigs becomes a matter of survival rather than choice. This transformation, from hopeful revolutionaries to oppressed subjects once more, serves as a powerful commentary on the cyclical nature of power and rebellion. And this is underscored by Napoleon's transformation from a revolutionary leader into a corrupt tyrant.

Where Structure Meets Theme

In *Animal Farm*, structure and theme are intertwined. While the story's arc, events, and character dynamics form its structure,

Orwell's choice of animals contributes much of the underlying meaning.

The pigs' intelligence and cunning allow them to maneuver themselves into positions of power, reshaping the farm's hierarchy. They are an elite class leveraging its knowledge and resources to exploit and dominate others. Their transformation from comrades-in-arms to rulers mimics the way leadership can evolve in political scenarios— the shift from espoused ideals into oppressive rule.

The sheep, on the other hand, epitomize the blind followers of any regime. Their incessant bleating of simplistic slogans like "Four legs good, two legs bad" serves as a metaphor for propaganda and the dangers of unthinking loyalty.

Boxer, the horse, stands as a tragic figure of the working class. His unwavering dedication, evidenced by his mottos, "I will work harder" and "Napoleon is always right," reflects the proletariat's exploitation. The eventual betrayal of Boxer is one of the story's most heart-wrenching moments and is emblematic of how totalitarian regimes often discard those who serve them once they're no longer useful.

The choice of animals thus isn't just a creative storytelling device. It's how Orwell invests the simplistic parable structure with thematic and allegorical depth.

Why Is *Animal Farm* a Classic?

Animal Farm is a wonderful demonstration of the versatility and boundless possibilities of storytelling. "Narrative" almost universally involves a protagonist struggling and striving toward a goal, the failure of which comes with significant stakes. It is the stakes that make readers care: the closer a protagonist gets to failure, the more readers cheer them on, the more they want to know what happens next.

But through this parable-like tale of Soviet communism, Orwell demonstrates that dramatic irony can be another potent tool to engage and sustain a reader's emotional draw. While most stories weave their magic through the interplay of character desires, stakes, and conflicts, Orwell's masterpiece thrives on readers' apprehension, their knowledge of the looming disaster, and their expectation of the tragic, inevitable descent of the hopeful revolutionaries. Stakes are still there, even without a singular protagonist fighting for their heart's desire.

Chapter Summary: Barnyard Betrayal

Animal Farm gives us commentary not only on history and political philosophy but also on the art of storytelling itself—demonstrating that narrative structure is a playground for innovation rather than a formula or paint-by-numbers approach to novel writing.

Orwell makes structural decisions for thematic reasons (much like Virginia Woolf), giving us a collective protagonist and choosing the antagonist as the story driver.

Dramatic Irony: Dramatic irony occurs when readers possess knowledge that the characters within the story do not. This discrepancy creates tension, anticipation, or humor, as we understand the implications of events while the characters remain oblivious. In *Animal Farm*, dramatic irony is a central device. The animals believe they are working toward a utopian society, unaware that the pigs are manipulating them for personal gain. Readers, however, recognize the signs of emerging tyranny. This awareness amplifies the tragedy of the animals' situation, as we witness their naive trust leading them back into oppression.

The one cost to using dramatic irony in your work is suspense. If readers can see more than the characters, they may already know (or think they know) what's going to happen. However, what they might not know is the *how* and the *why* of what will happen. This uncertainty keeps readers engaged, as they piece together the unfolding story and anticipate the consequences of the characters' actions. The challenge lies in revealing just enough to build tension while holding back enough to maintain intrigue.

Parable: A parable is a succinct allegorical story designed to convey a moral or philosophical lesson. It employs symbolism and metaphor to illustrate universal truths, often using simple narratives and characters to make complex ideas accessible. Parables focus less on detailed character development and more on the overarching message or teaching.

The risk with writing a parable is embedded in its definition: if you try too hard to instruct the reader, you might end up with a story that is preachy. But forewarned is forearmed. Aim for subtlety.

Satire: Satire is a literary technique that employs humor, irony, exaggeration, or ridicule to expose and criticize human follies, vices, or societal problems. Its purpose is often to provoke thought, inspire change, or highlight the absurdities within a culture or political system. Satire can be subtle or overt, but it always aims to reveal truths through wit.

George Orwell uses satire to critique the Russian Revolution and the subsequent rise of the Soviet Union under Stalin. By anthropomorphizing farm animals to represent political figures and classes, he exaggerates their traits to highlight the absurdity and hypocrisy of the regime. The pigs' gradual adoption of human behaviors mocks the corruption of socialist ideals.

Allegory: An allegory is a narrative in which characters, events, and settings symbolize abstract ideas or real-world occurrences, allowing the story to operate on both a literal and a symbolic level. Through this duality, allegories convey moral, ethical, or political commentary.

The Godfather

by Mario Puzo

Vito the Puppet Master

The Godfather, published in 1969, was Mario Puzo's breakthrough novel. It was met with both critical acclaim and commercial success, spending sixty-seven weeks on *The New York Times* Best Sellers list and selling over nine million copies in its first two years. Although the novel itself did not win any major literary awards, it had a significant impact on the genre of crime and Mafia fiction, influencing countless stories in literature, film, and television. Puzo cowrote the screenplay with director Francis Ford Coppola, and the adaptation won the Academy Award for Best Adapted Screenplay.

What is fascinating about this novel for our purposes is that it employs an "event" structure, wherein multiple character arcs revolve around a central incident—the attempted assassination of Vito Corleone and its aftermath. This event serves as the anchor for the various subplots, each character's journey intersecting and responding to this pivotal moment. Also, despite Vito's limited direct action throughout the novel, his influence permeates each subplot. He guides and nudges events from behind the scenes, always working toward his master plan, even after (spoiler alert) his own death. Vito's causality bleeds through the narrative, both in his role as the head of the family and as the guiding force behind each character's actions.

Narrative Goal

Vito Corleone, known as the Godfather, is a character shaped by a complex past of resilience, cunning, and calculated generosity. Having risen to power through strategic alliances and a firm sense of justice within the criminal underworld, he possesses an underlying motivation to secure a future in which his family can achieve both prosperity and stability—free from the volatility that often plagues those in his line of work. This desire to protect his family and ensure their continued success is the driving force behind his every action.

When Vito refuses to join a proposed narcotics operation, he unwittingly sets in motion a chain of events that threatens both his family's prosperity and their security. The assassination attempt on him acts as a catalyst, kicking off a broader power struggle and an impending drug war among New York's crime families. Faced with this looming threat, Vito makes long-term plans to secure his family's future, carefully orchestrating the actions of his sons and allies to ensure their survival and eventual dominance.

We can restate this more simply in logline form: After surviving an attempt on his life, Vito Corleone must secure his family's future amid escalating threats, strategically guiding his reluctant son Michael into the role of the next Godfather to ensure their legacy endures.

Stasis: What Vito Stands to Lose

The stasis in *The Godfather* is an extended sequence that serves to establish Vito Corleone's character, domain, and power, primarily through the perspectives of others. This is a classic example of demonstrating what the protagonist stands to lose. Vito's control and the family's prosperity seem unassailable, making it inevitable that this stability will soon come under threat.

The novel begins with two community members, the undertaker Bonasera and the baker Nazorine, each deciding that they need the Godfather's help. This opening establishes Vito's role as a figure of power and influence, someone to whom others turn when they have nowhere else to go.

Following these initial requests, we move into the wedding of Vito's daughter, Connie, where the Godfather continues to demonstrate his influence and control by granting favors to those who seek an audience with him. The wedding scene showcases the power dynamics within the Corleone family and Vito's ability to manage his criminal empire even amid a personal celebration. This scene is also where we meet Vito's three sons, each of whom will be tested over the course of the novel.

PLOT POINTS

The Godfather is a tapestry of plotlines. There are a number of what we could call minor protagonists, each at the helm of their own subplot; these include characters like Carlo Rizzi, Dr. Segal, and Tom Hagen—though Hagen is arguably Vito's avatar more than an active agent in his own right. But for the sake of this analysis, we will focus on the biggest players—Vito's three sons, along with his godson Johnny Fontane, who represents the Godfather's interests in Hollywood.

Vito Corleone's three sons—Sonny, Fredo, and Michael—are crucial to his goal of achieving family stability. Aware that his death will come sooner or later, Vito observes how each son responds to the crises that threaten the family. Through their individual actions and choices amid unfolding events, these plotlines reveal which son has what it takes to succeed him as the head of the family. At first, Sonny is the only one willing to lead, but he lacks cunning; Fredo has been learning the business and may have some cunning, but he is soft and hedonistic; Michael is loyal to the family but wants his own independence. While Fontane isn't in the line of succession, he is still integral to the plan; with Vito's muscle and money, he reestablishes his career in Hollywood and thereby provides the Godfather with a new line of investment and influence.

Let's take a closer look:

Johnny Fontane

Stasis

Johnny has lost his voice and his confidence. His wife has left him, and his second marriage is falling apart. He desperately wants a role in a major movie, but the director despises him and refuses to cast him.

Inciting Incident

Vito sends Tom Hagen to help Johnny get back on track. Hagen makes it clear that Johnny should trust in his godfather's power to solve his problems.

Johnny's goal is to revive his career in Hollywood. At first, he sees acting as a possible solution, but what he really wants is to be able to sing again.

Rising Action

Johnny faces obstacles in the form of powerful studio heads, particularly the director who refuses to cast him, and in his failing confidence, which has damaged his career. However, with Vito's help, Johnny gets a second chance at success. He reconciles with his ex-wife, secures the coveted acting role, and even wins an award for his performance. Eventually, Johnny meets a maverick surgeon allied with the family and undergoes an operation that restores his voice.

Climax

The surgery helps Johnny's voice somewhat, but it's not until he's able to fully take control of his life and recognize his worth, individually and as a member of the family, with the Don's full respect, that he regains the confidence he needs to sing. This culminates in Johnny cutting a new album after he thought his singing days were behind him forever.

Resolution

After successfully recording his new album, Johnny becomes integrated into the family's plans for Vegas, using his celebrity status to promote their growing interests in hotels and entertainment. He works alongside the Corleones to establish Las Vegas as both a gambling hub and an entertainment hot spot. His presence in Vegas helps draw celebrities and high-profile attention, boosting the Corleones' influence and providing Johnny with a more stable future, both as a performer and an ally to the family. This is part of Vito's plan to shift the family empire into a legal business and thus avoid the narcotics trade.

Santino "Sonny" Corleone

Stasis

During Vito's crucial first meeting about the drug trade, Sonny fails to guard his tongue; his outburst reveals both his impulsiveness and his desire for the family to get involved in the lucrative narcotics business. This moment demonstrates his bullheadedness and also creates a vulnerability within the Corleones, as the rival family boss, Virgil Sollozzo, sees a division he can exploit.

Inciting Incident

The assassination attempt on Vito serves as Sonny's inciting incident, forcing him to take charge of the family in his father's absence. Sonny's narrative goal is to lead the family and avenge the attempt on his father's life.

Rising Action

Sonny's leadership is marked by a rash and ruthless approach, resulting in a series of violent retaliations against rival families. He orders hits against those who were involved in the assassination attempt on Vito, escalating the conflict between the families. His aggressive and reckless nature leads to several successful but unsustainable victories, which ultimately draw significant resistance from the rival bosses. His approach lacks the strategic foresight of his father, leaving the family vulnerable.

Climax and Resolution

The climax occurs when Sonny rushes to help his sister, Connie, who is being abused by her husband, Carlo Rizzi. Sonny's impulsive nature prevents him from considering the possibility that Carlo, a man willing to abuse a Corleone daughter, might also be capable of betraying the family. Thus Sonny falls into a trap; Carlo has tipped off a rival family, leading to Sonny's death in a brutal ambush at a tollbooth. This tragic ending underscores Sonny's inability to lead with the cunning and patience necessary to protect the Corleone family. He has failed his test.

Fredo Corleone

Fredo's plotline culminates in a series of failures that demonstrate his inability to lead even in a limited capacity. However, we don't see too much of him. The omniscient narrator instead favors Michael, Sonny, and Johnny. We learn about Fredo's trials through other characters, like Dr. Segal and later Michael, as well as through rumors of the Godfather's displeasure with his middle child.

Stasis

During the assassination attempt on Vito, Fredo reacts badly, dropping his gun and collapsing in shock. This failure demonstrates his weakness of character and shows that he lacks the "Sicilian balls" required to be a leader in the family.

Inciting Incident

Later, Vito sends Fredo to Las Vegas to work with Moe Greene. This move is Fredo's inciting incident, giving him a fresh opportunity to prove himself. However, Fredo is mainly concerned with having a good time and getting laid, which makes him a reluctant protagonist—he does not actively pursue the quest that his father has given him.

Rising Action

During his time in Las Vegas, Fredo spends his days sleeping around—often with multiple women—and allowing Moe Greene to call the shots. He fails to effectively represent the family's interests in the hotel venture.

Climax

In a flagrant display of disrespect, Moe Greene slaps Fredo in public, and Fredo does nothing to stand up to him.

Resolution

Ultimately, Fredo is a failure. Vito is forced to send Michael to Vegas to take control and move forward with the family's plan to transition into the more legitimate business of hotels and gambling. Fredo's inability to succeed underscores his role as the weakest link among Vito's sons.

Michael Corleone

In the vast majority of novels, the protagonist is the main character. But there are exceptions. For example, in *The Great Gatsby* and *Moby-Dick*, the narrator is not the protagonist, and since we spend the most "page time" with the narrator, they can be said to be the main character, even if they aren't driving the plot. In *The Godfather*, Vito is arguably the principal protagonist since he impacts and steers the plotlines of all the other characters. However, Michael is the main character. Over the course of the novel, we get to know him the best, and his development plays out across three distinct arcs.

1) Accepting His Destiny

Stasis

The initial stasis and inciting incident take place before the novel opens. We don't learn about the specific moment or event that causes Michael to desire a life outside of the Corleone Mafia world, but that is the narrative goal he is working toward at the beginning of the story.

Point of No Return

This also takes place before page one. Michael attends college and, more importantly, enlists and does a tour in the military—against his father's wishes. He has made it abundantly clear that he will forge his own way in the world.

Rising Action

This is where the novel opens. Michael is courting Kay, a Yankee woman, to whom he explains at his sister's wedding that his family is "different." We get the sense that he also sees himself as different and outside the family business, though he is still fiercely loyal to his father and won't divulge much to Kay.

Midpoint Reversal

The assassination attempt on his father marks a turning point for Michael. In terms of his want-versus-need dichotomy, he *wants* independence from the family, but he *needs* to remain loyal. Loyalty is at the core of who he is. Thus, his narrative goal changes at this point. He gives up on his *want* in order to accept his *need*. In Vito's words, he has found his true destiny. He will protect his family, and this means stepping into his role within the Corleone empire.

Rising Action

Michael initially gets involved by trying to assist Sonny in managing the family's affairs, though Sonny resists his brother's help and tries to sideline him. Michael then steps up to protect Vito when the brothers realize there is a new threat at the hospital; he risks his own safety to move his father to a secure location. During this incident, a corrupt police officer, Captain McCluskey, punches Michael in the face, which leads Michael to propose a plan to eliminate McCluskey and the rival boss Sollozzo. This pivotal decision marks Michael's commitment to the family—he insists on executing the hit himself.

Climax

Michael goes to an Italian restaurant to meet with Sollozzo and Captain McCluskey under the guise of negotiating peace. During the meeting, Michael retrieves a hidden gun from the restroom and murders both Sollozzo and McCluskey. This act is his definitive break from his previous life and solidifies his commitment to the family's path of violence and power.

Resolution

Michael has fully stepped into the family's world, abandoning his previous aspirations and accepting his destiny as part of the Corleone crime family. He must also walk away from his relationship with Kay. Vito arranges to smuggle him out of the country and keep him in hiding until they can clear his name. Michael has sacrificed all his life goals, but in doing so, he has shifted the balance of power back in favor of the Corleone family.

2) Michael's Italian Romance

Stasis

After the murder of Sollozzo and McCluskey, Michael is sent to Sicily to hide. Here he has a general goal of "biding his time" in Italy, waiting for the day when he can return to his family in New York.

Inciting Incident

Michael falls in love with Apollonia at first sight: he is struck by "the thunderbolt."

Even though Michael is meant to lie low in Italy, he cannot ignore the thunderbolt. He begins courting Apollonia, knowing that doing so will raise his profile in Sicily.

Rising Action and False Victory

In order to win Apollonia's hand, Michael must first convince her parents of his worthiness. He does so with grace and generosity, and soon he and Apollonia are married.

Tragic Climax

Apollonia is killed in a car bomb meant for Michael. Her death is a critical turning point that fuels in him the ruthlessness and resolve he will need to survive the world of the Mafia.

Resolution

Apollonia's death sets Michael on a path of vengeance and ambition as he returns to the United States. This episode solidifies his commitment to defeating the family's enemies. In getting to know Michael's capacity for love and loyalty, readers are able to connect with him more deeply, and we are also primed to accept his brutality to come. We see in him the compassion and vulnerability that Sonny lacks. However, that compassion and vulnerability are now tempered. He has learned an important lesson: his willingness to draw attention to himself in winning Apollonia's hand is what brought his enemies down upon him.

3) The Next Godfather

Stasis

Michael returns from Sicily and takes on more responsibility within the family. He is now well positioned as Vito's successor.

Inciting Incident

Vito formally steps back, preparing Michael to take over as head of the family. Michael's goal is to consolidate power, eliminate threats to the Corleone family, and establish himself as the new Don.

Rising Action

Michael orchestrates a series of strategic moves, including relocating the family's operations to Las Vegas and leading the rival families to believe the Corleones have grown weak under the youngest son's leadership. Also, while Michael assumed Kay wouldn't want to have anything to do with him and his crime family, she has awaited his return. They marry, but he makes it clear that they will never discuss the family business.

Climax

Michael eliminates a number of significant rivals and traitors in a sweeping, ruthless move, asserting his dominance as the new Don. This includes orchestrating the murder of his brother-in-law Carlo, as well as taking out longtime ally Salvatore Tessio, who betrayed Vito's trust by conspiring with the Barzini family against the Corleones.

Resolution

Michael secures his position as the new head of the Corleone family, but at great personal cost. He has transformed into a figure even more ruthless than his father, giving up on his initial desire for independence, losing much of his humanity, and becoming isolated from those he loves, including his wife. However, since we have accompanied him through all of these trials, we have empathy for his evolution—we can see his justification for the path he has taken.

Michael Is the Next Vito

In the foreword to *The Godfather*, Francis Ford Coppola mentions that Vito Corleone's three sons each represent different aspects of their father. Coppola saw this as a key element of the story, with each son inheriting distinct characteristics. This thematic approach helped him craft the film by emphasizing these traits: Sonny's fiery aggression, Fredo's vulnerability, and Michael's combination of intelligence and determination.

However, we disagree with Coppola's assessment. In taking on Sollozzo and McCluskey, Michael shows that he has Sonny's fiery aggression. In his Italian romance with Apollonia and marriage to Kay, he demonstrates his compassion and vulnerability. And he has what the other two lack: patience and cunning. In our reading of the text, Sonny and Fredo represent partial reflections of their father, but without the full package, neither is fit to lead. Over the course of the story, Michael proves that he has what it takes to replace the Godfather. He is the rightful heir.

The White Lotus Critique

In the second season of *White Lotus*, an HBO show written and directed by Mike White and set in a resort in Sicily, there is a brief discussion about *The Godfather*. One of the characters, Albie Di Grasso, critiques the novel as being sexist, while his grandfather, Bert, defends it as a product of its time. Since we watched this series right before reading the book, we brought this question into our analysis.

It's true that there is a lot of misogyny and violence against the women in the novel, and it's reasonable to assume this is a fair take on the gender dynamics of the time. However, a sexist representation does not necessarily equate to a sexist narrative. For example, many authors depict sexism and misogyny as part of a cultural or societal critique. Yet there doesn't seem to be any such critique here. Further, none of the women in the story are afforded narrative agency; that is to say, they are characterized by their relationships to men, and not through their own desires or ambitions.

In Sicily, Apollonia is beautiful and demure. Through her, we witness Michael's tenderness, and her death becomes a lesson that solidifies his resolve. Beyond that, Vito's daughter Connie is used to reveal Carlo Rizzi's villainy. Sonny's mistress Lucy is a window into Sonny's divergence from Vito's code of ethics. Later, her condition of pelvic relaxation provides a means for the family-allied Dr. Jules Segal to prove his worth, which leads to him diagnosing Johnny Fontane's throat condition and connecting the singer with a specialist. While Vito's wife Carmela (Mama Corleone) helps Michael reconnect with Kay after his time in Sicily, she is largely an anchor for Vito, attending church regularly to pray for her sinful husband. Of all the women in *The Godfather*, Kay comes closest to having an arc, and yet it is still based around her longing to be with Michael.

While he is in Sicily, she waits patiently for him to return. When the secrecy of his new role in the family strains their relationship, she quietly accepts the distance between them. And finally, once they are married and Michael has taken over the family business, she assumes Carmela's role as anchor—she converts to Catholicism so she too can pray for her sinful husband.

Apart from their relationships to the central characters, not one of the female characters has a narrative goal of her own. This isn't to suggest they should have active roles within the Mafia itself, but even in limited roles, characters can have personal motivations and inner lives. In this novel, the women feel more like devices than living, breathing characters, which is stark when you consider the depth of characterization Puzo affords the men. Just as the women are objects of possession for their men, so they are similarly the author's tools for plot and characterization.

Why Is *The Godfather* a Classic?

One of the central themes of *The Godfather* is destiny. Vito Corleone speaks to this when he says, "Many young men started down a false path to their true destiny. Time and fortune usually set them aright." This sentiment clearly applies to Michael. Despite his efforts to carve out an independent life, the trials he faces—beginning with the assassination attempt on his father—pull him back in, ultimately setting him on the path to lead the Corleone family.

Yet what makes *The Godfather* so compelling is how destiny is not left to chance alone. Vito, as the godfather of both crime and plot, actively shapes the destinies of many. His long-term schemes, his plan to protect and groom Michael, and even his influence from beyond the grave, all ensure that Michael steps into his role as his father's successor. In the end, Michael's journey is not just about accepting his fate; it is about the inevitability of Vito's influence, demonstrating that destiny is often inescapable precisely because it is guided by those who wield power.

The cultural impact of *The Godfather* has been magnified by its film adaptation. The movie, cowritten by Mario Puzo and Francis Ford Coppola, helped cement the novel's legacy. Coppola's film brought the story to a wider audience and elevated it to an iconic status, no doubt one of the most influential films of all time. The success of the film has ensured that the Corleones' saga remains a timeless piece of both literary and cinematic history.

Chapter Summary: An Offer You Can't Refuse

Vito Corleone is a godfather of crime, but he is also a godfather of plot. While some might chalk this book up to a swashbuckling adventure of crime and revenge, it is a structural masterpiece. What's most unusual here is that the protagonist, Vito, is not the main character. The main action revolves around Michael. While other co-protagonists have a single plot arc, Michael has three. The novel is his origin story. But at the heart of it all is Vito, pulling the strings, laying traps, and positioning his crime family in a long-term scheme that, in the end, has them best their enemies and set the Corleone clan up for a secure future in Las Vegas. Even toward the end, when Michael is feasibly running the show, he is using his father's playbook, and the actions he takes after Vito's death are still part of the plan Vito was working toward all along.

Main Character Versus Protagonist: The terms *main character* and *protagonist* are usually synonymous, but it's possible for them to represent distinct roles within a narrative. The protagonist is the central figure who drives the plot forward through their actions, desires, and decisions. They are the primary agent of change, facing obstacles and pursuing goals that shape the story's trajectory. The main character, however, is the character through whose perspective the story is told. This character is the lens for the audience, providing insight, narration, or emotional connection to the events unfolding.

In *The Godfather*, Vito Corleone is the protagonist whose actions and plans drive the overarching narrative. His strategic decisions shape the destinies of those around him. Michael Corleone, his youngest son, is the main character through whom we experience much of the story. (The narrator, however, is omniscient.)

Event Structure: An event structure is a narrative framework in which multiple characters' individual storylines and arcs are interconnected through a central event or series of events. It's commonly used in stories where a major incident—such as a disaster, war, or competition—serves as the focal point around which personal and collective dramas unfold.

In event structures, the central event acts as a catalyst that triggers the characters' journeys. It can be the inciting incident that sets the plot in motion or a known climactic eventuality that brings storylines together. Multiple arcs develop as each character responds to the event in their own way.

Examples include disaster stories where an impending catastrophe forces diverse characters to interact and work together, or sports narratives where team members strive toward victory in a crucial game. In *The Godfather*, the attempted assassination of Vito Corleone serves as the central event that ties together the various character arcs.

Middlemarch

by George Eliot

An Orchestra of a Novel

Middlemarch has been hailed as the greatest British novel ever written (although apparently, if you Google *I hate Middlemarch*, you will discover kindred spirits on Facebook). Virginia Woolf described it as "one of the few English novels written for grown-up people." It's a brick of a book, the kind you look at and think, *how will I ever get through it?* But once you're in the middle of it, you'll find yourself wishing it would never end. It's a novel you want to live in. Truly, this is a masterpiece of both characterization and structure. How George Eliot wrote it without going absolutely mad is something we'd like to know, but the way she plants so many seeds early in the novel convinces us she must have planned it out meticulously.

George Eliot is the pen name of Mary Ann Evans. She wrote as a man so that she would be taken seriously. Even so, most people already knew she was a woman from her previous work, and *Middlemarch* was criticized as being "depressing" and "too intellectual" for a female novelist—no doubt the very criticisms she had hoped to avoid.

The novel is set in the fictional town of Middlemarch and takes place from 1829–1832. It begins with several separate storylines that slowly but surely intertwine, all under the able guidance of a very vocal narrator, much like an orchestra with its sections of woodwinds, strings, brass, percussion—and a conductor who keeps it all in order.

This is not a typical novel because there is not a singular protagonist. While Dorothea Brooke's story begins and ends the novel, and while the first inciting incident belongs to her, there are so many different characters and storylines, each with their own inciting incidents, it's hard to argue for Dorothea as the main character. Instead, Middlemarch itself—or rather, provincial life in this typical English town—forms the beating heart of the novel.

There's also no real antagonist. Casaubon might be considered one for a while, as might Bulstrode, but Eliot also makes them sympathetic. The real antagonist in the novel is the relentless process of change and people's general resistance to it.

Because Eliot was in the vanguard of the realistic novel, she aims to portray life the way it really is (like Flaubert), rather than giving us the romantic version typical of many novelists at the time. Instead of marriage marking the end of the novel in a happily-ever-after scenario, marriage is where the story begins. As a result, shit gets real in a hurry. We get to watch the romantic courtships and idealized notions of various significant others, and then we see how things fall apart under the heavy and unrelenting weight of reality.

Every so often the town itself gets a plot point—with regard to politics or the organization of the hospital or the coming railway. Through the town and its inhabitants, Eliot shows us the social dynamics and pressures of the time, the politics and gossip, the change that was in the air and how so many people were discomfited by it. It's as though she holds a camera and occasionally pans out to give us the bigger picture, then zooms back in on the main characters. She uses the crowd like a Greek chorus, providing commentary both on what's going on generally and in reference to the characters we're familiar with.

PLOT POINTS

The novel is divided into eight books (which is how it was published), but there are four main storylines (with numerous others that feed into them):

- Dorothea Brooke with Edward Casaubon and Will Ladislaw
- Tertius Lydgate with Rosamond Vincy and Nicholas Bulstrode
- Fred Vincy with Mary Garth and Mr. Farebrother
- Nicholas Bulstrode and his secret and scandalous past

Bits and pieces of these various storylines appear in nearly every book. Many of the storylines happen concurrently, almost as though we are peering down on the town from above and watching the stories unfold in different places.

Middlemarch might be long, but Eliot demonstrates that every plot point exists for a reason and will reap a harvest somewhere in the future. Nothing is superfluous. Nothing exists for its own sake without follow-up or causality. She also makes great use of fatal flaws in each of her main characters.

Let's break down these narrative trajectories.

Dorothea Brooke

Dorothea is a key character both in the plot of *Middlemarch* and thematically, as a woman with great potential who never really gets the chance to fulfill it. She is also stubborn, and it is her stubbornness that gets her into trouble, and her triumph over it that allows her to (sort of) achieve her narrative goal.

Stasis

Dorothea longs to do something serious with her life, though as a woman her opportunities are limited. Her eye is on the tenant cottages on her uncle's property that need improvement, but her uncle isn't much interested in that.

Inciting Incident

The clergyman and scholar Edward Casaubon proposes marriage. He is much older than Dorothea, but she envisions marriage to him as a path to a serious intellectual life. She wants to help him with his book, *The Key to All Mythologies*, the great project of his life. Everyone thinks the marriage is a mistake and that she should marry the younger and more attractive Sir James Chettam instead (which would also be a mistake). But because Dorothea is headstrong and idealistic, she accepts Casaubon's proposal. Her narrative goal is to be of use to him, specifically in the writing of his book.

Rising Action

Eliot doesn't wait for the honeymoon to be over before bursting Dorothea's bubble. Casaubon turns out to be distant and cold, and Dorothea is often left alone with nothing to do. While in Rome, she runs into Casaubon's much younger cousin, Will Ladislaw, which begins an important friendship that causes unintended jealousy. The contrast between the young and attractive Ladislaw and old, crotchety Casaubon couldn't be greater. She soon realizes that Casaubon's project is too unwieldy to be realistic and is doomed to remain unfinished. Casaubon senses her doubt in him, and this, coupled with his jealousy over Ladislaw's repeated visits, creates insecurity.

Midpoint Reversal

After suffering some heart trouble (and being treated by the new doctor, Tertius Lydgate), Casaubon drops dead, and Dorothea suddenly finds herself a widow with a huge inheritance and one surprising catch in the will: if she marries Ladislaw, she must forfeit her inheritance. She is enraged by this assumption of wrongdoing on her part. Not only does she vow never to remarry (allowing her stubbornness to get in the way again), but she also refuses to finish *The Key to All Mythologies*, thus giving up on this form of her narrative goal.

Rising Action

Despite the codicil in Casaubon's will, Dorothea's feelings for Ladislaw grow. But she resists them, partly because she doesn't want to go against Casaubon's wishes, but also partly because of her stubborn streak. When Ladislaw suggests he will leave Middlemarch (hoping she'll beg him to stay), she says nothing. New rumors fly around town that Ladislaw has been spending time with Rosamond.

In the meantime, Dorothea gets involved with the new hospital by donating money and thereby having a hand in the meaningful social reform she yearned for. When she hears the rumor that Lydgate accepted a bribe from the hospital founder, Nicholas Bulstrode, and might be implicated in the death of a stranger named John Raffles, she refuses to believe it.

All Is Lost

She offers to cover Lydgate's debts, but when she arrives at his house to deliver the check, she walks in on Rosamond and Ladislaw holding hands. Misunderstanding the scene, she rushes out, believing all is lost with Ladislaw. Her emotions are more powerful than her stubbornness. She can no longer deny her feelings for him and realizes that maybe she deserves to be happy. Eliot gives us a late reversal here: despite Dorothea's best efforts, her narrative goal has shifted; she wants to marry Ladislaw.

Climax

She finally overcomes her stubbornness, decides to take the high road, and returns to Rosamond to tell her about her support of Lydgate. Rosamond admits the truth: Ladislaw has only ever loved Dorothea. Dorothea and Ladislaw declare their love for each other and decide to marry even though Dorothea will have to forfeit Casaubon's inheritance.

Resolution

Dorothea and Ladislaw have a happy married life together, and though she never does the reform work she originally dreamed of, she does support medical reform in Middlemarch and achieves her goal of marrying Ladislaw. And she overcomes her fatal flaw.

Tertius Lydgate

Lydgate is another key character in a separate storyline that intersects Dorothea's in several places. As the new surgeon in town, he serves an important structural purpose. Eliot uses him to weave various storylines together, since many of the characters become his patients. Lydgate, however, will be dogged by a pride that creates dangerous arrogance through most of the novel.

Stasis

Lydgate arrives in Middlemarch eager to make a name for himself in medicine. He has come from Paris, where he left behind a disastrous love affair, and brings with him some newfangled ideas about studying anatomy and treating disease.

Inciting Incident

Lydgate secures the position of physician at the newly established Fever Hospital, supported by the influential but morally questionable banker, Nicholas Bulstrode. This position offers him a platform for his medical reforms with regard to modern treatments (his narrative goal), though the townsfolk of Middlemarch aren't fond of new ideas.

Point of No Return

Rosamond Vincy has her eye on Lydgate before he starts paying attention to her. It is her brother Fred Vincy's illness that causes Lydgate to spend more time at the Vincy home—where, against his better judgment, he consequently spends more time with Rosamond. Eventually Lydgate proposes to Rosamond, not seeing beyond her physical attributes, and she accepts. Marriage to Rosamond will become Lydgate's biggest obstacle to achieving his goal, and it is a direct result of pride. She's pretty and elegant, and she's the mayor's daughter. He figures she'll look good at his side.

Rising Action

Lydgate wants to make changes to the medical system, but his arrogance when it comes to dealing with small-town people makes him bullheaded and insensitive. It doesn't take long for him to start making enemies all over town on both a personal and professional level. To make matters worse, Rosamond is high-maintenance and not easy to live with. In order to keep her happy, Lydgate spends more than he should to rent and furnish their house.

Midpoint Reversal

Because Lydgate is too proud to admit the truth about their finances, Rosamond continues to spend money. It's clear to both of them that this marriage was a mistake, but they're stuck in it. Instead of focusing on medical reforms, Lydgate must now deal with his mounting debts.

Rising Action

Lydgate can no longer hide his debts. He finally tells Rosamond they will have to move to a smaller house, but she manipulates things so that it can't happen and goes behind his back to ask his relatives for money—and they refuse. At his wits' end, he resorts to gambling and is narrowly rescued from ruin by Fred Vincy. He then approaches Bulstrode to ask for a loan. Bulstrode refuses, suggesting he should declare bankruptcy.

False Victory

When Bulstrode changes his mind and offers Lydgate the loan, Lydgate doesn't realize that the timing will make it look like a bribe. The offer of money comes just before John Raffles dies, and Lydgate is the doctor who treats him. He has no idea about Bulstrode's nefarious past, nor does he know that Raffles is blackmailing Bulstrode—and of course he cannot guess that Bulstrode will have a hand in Raffles' death.

But he also doesn't ask many questions. He believes his money problems are over. He won't have to move to a smaller home and endure Rosamond's complaints about being poor. His pride and social standing are intact. He can continue with his medical reforms, as planned.

Tragic Climax

Lydgate becomes implicated in the scandal surrounding Bulstrode, who is exposed both for the questionable source of his wealth and his involvement in the death of Raffles—which many suspect was a murder. So much for his pride. Lydgate faces public humiliation and the collapse of his professional dreams, but Dorothea steps in to clear his name and offer him money so that he can return Bulstrode's loan. Her actions are as much a reflection of her own character as they are an endorsement of his attempts at medical reform. They also fulfill her narrative goal of actively supporting reform.

It is noteworthy that Lydgate helps Bulstrode out of the town meeting in which the latter is publicly humiliated—at the direct expense of Lydgate's reputation. Here is the demonstration of his arc: he must swallow his pride to support a man who has been vilified by the community.

Resolution

Lydgate's story is a tragedy. Thanks to the Bulstrode scandal, the damage to his reputation is significant. He can only salvage his medical practice by moving to London, and he sort of salvages his marriage. He and Rosamond are never really happy, and he dies young without ever achieving his true goal. But he does overcome his fatal flaw.

Fred Vincy

Fred's trajectory is different from the other characters who start off with big ambitions and then careen downhill. He starts in the dumps—and things get worse before they get better—but his journey is from irresponsibility to maturity, driven by his love for Mary Garth and his desire to earn her respect. In this way, he can be considered an antihero. His fatal flaw is that he's lazy.

Stasis

When the novel begins, Fred is a bit of a dilettante. He's failed his exam at college and is deeply in debt but assumes he'll be rescued when he inherits his elderly (and ill) uncle's fortune. His narrative goal is to make something of himself so that Mary Garth will marry him. But he starts the novel by going about it the wrong way: trusting in luck and his inheritance and doing the least amount of work possible. His strategy is guaranteed to fail, since Mary comes from a family founded on the value of hard work. She has known him since childhood, and though she loves him, she sees his flaws clearly and won't marry him until he overcomes them.

Inciting Incident

Fred borrows money to buy a horse and convinces Mary's father, Caleb, to cosign on the debt he owes, figuring it's not a huge risk. He'll sell the horse for more than he bought it for and thereby win Mary's hand.

Rising Action

Fred trusts in luck, and luck lets him down. The horse he buys goes lame, Fred loses everything, and the Garth family can't afford to cover his losses without sacrificing their savings (including Mary's). Stressed from the loss, Fred gets sick.

Midpoint

When Uncle Featherstone finally dies, the will reveals that Fred stands to receive nothing. Mary refuses to marry him unless he becomes serious about a vocation. Her encouragement—along with Mr. Vincy's insistence that Fred go back to school to finish his theology degree—sets him on the long road to a responsible life. Rather than trusting to luck to make his fortune, he must learn to work for it. As is typical of an antihero, Fred must overcome his flaw at the midpoint.

Rising Action

Fred finishes school but abandons the idea of joining the clergy. Instead, he starts working with Caleb Garth, learning agricultural work and estate management. A new threat enters in the form of Mr. Farebrother as a rival for Mary's hand, but Mary makes it clear that she loves Fred and won't give him up for anyone else.

All Is Lost

In a classic "recovering addict" moment, Fred shows up at the Green Dragon, his former gambling haunt. As a reformed gambler, he figures he won't be tempted to bet. Naturally, he's wrong. He is tempted—until he sees Lydgate there, which shocks him back to his senses. When Mr. Farebrother threatens to court Mary if he starts gambling again, Fred vows never to go back down that road. He must continue to choose hard work over luck.

Climax

To make things up to his wife (who is a Vincy), Bulstrode arranges for Caleb Garth to manage Stone Court and for Fred to live there, and thus Mary consents to marry him. This is a nice reversal for Fred, since it's his own hard work that has earned him this stroke of so-called luck.

Resolution

Fred and Mary have a happy life together and raise three sons. This is one of the few happy marriages in the novel, probably because the couple knew each other for years before they got married and didn't have any idealistic notions about what they were getting into. Mary provided the motivation for Fred to overcome his fatal flaw.

Nicholas Bulstrode

Bulstrode's storyline is noteworthy because it doesn't really get off the ground until Book Five. In the meantime, Eliot plants seeds, making sure to introduce him in Book One and weaving him into the earlier books as a financial (and moralistic) presence in Middlemarch. By the time his story starts in earnest, we're prepared for it. Bulstrode is a hypocrite who believes he will never be found out.

Stasis

Bulstrode is the successful and moralistic banker in town who has his fingers in a lot of pies in terms of both the hospital and politics. He has an unsavory (but mysterious) past and is determined that no one will find out about it. He is therefore keen to protect his reputation and social standing in the town.

When Joshua Rigg inherits Mr. Featherstone's property and fortune, Bulstrode purchases Stone Court from him. More property means more influence and more protection from any suspicion that he came by his money dishonestly.

Inciting Incident

The purchase of Stone Court is how Rigg's stepfather, John Raffles, ends up in Middlemarch. While visiting Rigg, he spots a letter addressed to Bulstrode regarding this purchase and pockets it in the hopes of finding Bulstrode's address.

Raffles arrives to speak to Bulstrode, and Bulstrode offers him money to leave Middlemarch and never return. This is our first indication that Bulstrode is not the man we thought he was. Raffles poses a direct obstacle to Bulstrode's goal of cementing his influence in Middlemarch, and from this point on, Bulstrode's narrative goal becomes silencing or getting rid of Raffles.

What Raffles knows that no one else does is that Bulstrode came by his fortune dishonestly and the person to whom it actually should have gone was none other than Ladislaw's mother (and therefore Ladislaw). Raffles was the person Bulstrode hired to find Ladislaw's mother, and then he bribed him to keep quiet about it so that Bulstrode could keep the fortune. If Raffles lets this spill, Bulstrode's reputation in Middlemarch will be ruined.

Rising Action

Raffles starts to get around. He crosses paths with Ladislaw at an auction, stops in to visit Mrs. Bulstrode, and then heads to the bank to blackmail Bulstrode.

Midpoint

Realizing that he won't be able to shake Raffles, Bulstrode meets Ladislaw and tells him *part* of the truth, essentially offering to buy Ladislaw off. But Ladislaw senses this is dirty money and refuses it.

Rising Action

Lydgate approaches Bulstrode to ask for a loan. Bulstrode refuses, suggesting he should declare bankruptcy. Bulstrode is planning to leave town for a while and intends for Caleb Garth to manage Stone Court in his absence. Caleb plans to give the job to Fred Vincy, but when he finds Raffles at Stone Court, very ill, he backs out of the deal, suspecting something sketchy is going on.

Bulstrode allows Raffles to stay and calls for Lydgate, who says his illness is the result of alcoholism. He'll probably be fine as long as no one gives him anything more to drink. Bulstrode now changes his mind about the loan and agrees to give Lydgate the money.

False Victory

When Lydgate arrives the next morning to check on his patient, Raffles is dead. What Lydgate doesn't know is that Bulstrode allowed the housekeeper to take over watching Raffles, and when Raffles begged for brandy, Bulstrode gave the housekeeper the key to the liquor cabinet—knowing full well what would happen. However, Bulstrode believes no one is the wiser. No one has found out about his disreputable past. Silencing Raffles has allowed him to retain his influence in Middlemarch. It seems like he has attained his narrative goal.

Tragic Climax

Surprise. He's wrong. Rumors in Middlemarch spread faster than the plague. When Bulstrode goes to a town meeting, he discovers that *everyone* knows. He is forced to resign from all his public positions and leave the meeting in disgrace. Then his wife learns the truth. His hypocrisy has been revealed to all.

Resolution

Bulstrode is certain his wife will leave him. Instead, she wants him to make amends. Caleb Garth won't do business with him anymore, so he suggests she approach Caleb with the original offer to manage Stone Court and install Fred Vincy there, thus allowing Fred to marry Mary Garth. Bulstrode is ruined by the past that he sought to hide. He loses his social standing, but his wife remains loyal to him.

Bulstrode's transformation of character is harder to discern, but it is implied by the fact that he believes his wife should leave him—it's what he deserves—and yet she doesn't. Her loyalty suggests that he's worth staying for. Given his public humiliation, it's hard to imagine him doing the same thing again if he had the opportunity. But Eliot leaves that open to interpretation.

Idealizations Versus Reality

A lot of what Eliot does in this novel involves showing us the difference between our impressions and idealizations and what occurs when the scales fall from our eyes. It happens to nearly every main character.

- Dorothea sees Casaubon as a wise, accomplished scholar destined to achieve greatness with *The Key to All Mythologies*. Reality: he's a jealous, cold, and insecure old man whose ambition will never be realized.

- Casaubon sees Dorothea as an attractive, submissive, and devoted young woman—the perfect bride. Reality: she is smart, stubborn, and independent-minded, with her own ideas that don't necessarily mesh with his.
- Rosamond sees Lydgate as a successful and handsome aristocratic doctor who is guaranteed to provide her with the elegant lifestyle she craves. Reality: he has very little money and a tendency to rub people the wrong way with his arrogance, and he has little patience for Rosamond's idiosyncrasies.
- Lydgate sees Rosamond as a beautiful, pliant trophy wife—the perfect accessory. Reality: she is shallow and self-centered, spends too much money, and tries to manipulate him.
- The townspeople view Bulstrode as a successful and pious banker. Reality: his success is built on dishonesty, and his piousness is pure hypocrisy.

There are two main characters who do not idealize each other: Fred Vincy and Mary Garth. They have known each other since childhood and are not deceived by any false impressions. Mary recognizes that Fred is lazy and irresponsible, but she believes in his ability to improve himself—and indeed won't marry him until he does. Fred respects Mary's integrity, but he also recognizes that she doesn't have the social standing that his parents would prefer.

The Narrator

Like Jane Austen and Gustave Flaubert, Eliot experiments with free indirect discourse to give the reader more direct access to the characters' thoughts and emotions. But rather than being a neutral observer, the narrator of *Middlemarch* is a separate and rather vocal character who often addresses the reader with her commentary and insights. This was groundbreaking in its time.

The narrator forms a bond with the reader, sometimes using a conversational tone and even first-person POV, sometimes stepping back to offer her own ideas or opinions about what's going on. It feels very much like Eliot's voice.

Indeed, in Chapter Twenty-Nine, Eliot directly breaks the fourth wall: "One morning, some weeks after her arrival at Lowick, Dorothea—but why always Dorothea? Was her point of view the only possible one with regard to this marriage? ... Mr. Casaubon had an intense consciousness within him, and was spiritually a-hungered like the rest of us."

Not only does she remind us that we're reading a story, but she proceeds to shift the focus of the chapter to Casaubon.

Overall, the narrator is honest about the characters, and in the process, she forces us to take a closer look at ourselves—at marriage, at expectations and gossip, at how we idealize people we don't know well, and how we resist change.

Why Is *Middlemarch* a Classic?

Originally, Eliot was working on two separate novels, one about a doctor named Lydgate and the other about Dorothea. In a flash of brilliance, she decided to intertwine them into one great work of fiction.

Why is this book a classic? Because of the dialogue of Mrs. Cadwallader and Mr. Brooke. Because of the complexities of both the structure and the characters. Because Eliot doesn't shy away from the truth of human nature. Every character is a web of motivations, virtues, and flaws. They feel so real, they could walk in the door and you'd recognize them. This book is a tour de force, the sort of novel you can come back to again and again and find more things to admire in it—which is the definition of timelessness.

Chapter Summary: Characters in Concert

Middlemarch offers us a variety of interwoven storylines, where each main character has an arc but there is no single protagonist or antagonist. Instead, it's a snapshot of an entire town, of life in all its complexities—offered to us through the voice of a narrator who is a character in her own right.

Eliot manages this by careful plotting and foreshadowing, and by giving each main character a tragic flaw that forms their largest obstacle and that they must somehow overcome.

Nothing Superfluous: Every element within a narrative should serve a purpose, whether that's advancing the plot, developing characters, or reinforcing themes. In a densely packed novel, it's crucial that characters, events, and descriptions are not merely there as filler but contribute meaningfully to the overall story. This approach ensures coherence and keeps readers engaged, as each component adds value and drives the narrative forward.

George Eliot exemplifies this principle by intricately weaving multiple storylines and a large cast of characters into a cohesive whole. Despite the novel's complexity and length, every subplot and minor character plays a significant role in illustrating the social fabric of the town and the thematic explorations of ambition, love, and societal change. Eliot doesn't introduce characters or events arbitrarily; everything interconnects. Every detail is an investment that will pay dividends at a later point.

Plot Is Character: F. Scott Fitzgerald's assertion that "plot is character, character is plot" highlights the inseparable relationship between a story's events and the people who inhabit it. There are many characters in the mix in *Middlemarch*, and more plotlines than we've outlined in this Skeleton. The crucial takeaway is that plot demonstrates character, and that's why it's important for even minor characters to have their own perspective, goal, stakes, and transformation, even if subtle. *Middlemarch* shows how this can be done even in the midst of great complexity.

Breaking the Fourth Wall: *Breaking the fourth wall* refers to a narrative technique in which a character or the narrator addresses the audience directly, acknowledging the artificiality of the story. The term originates from theater, where the "fourth wall" is the imaginary barrier between actors and the audience. George Eliot employs this technique through a vocal and often intrusive narrator who directly addresses the reader. The narrator offers personal commentary, poses rhetorical questions, and provides insights that go beyond the characters' perspectives.

Wuthering Heights

by Emily Brontë

A Game of Names

Emily Brontë's *Wuthering Heights* promises not only to haunt readers long after they finish it, but it also has a complex narrative structure and mode of narration that are worthy of analysis. It has been described as both a gothic novel and a love story. The gothic part becomes evident pretty quickly. The love story is more like a cautionary tale: What happens when love is thwarted and becomes selfish and all-consuming? What happens when people are treated badly? Passion, it seems, has a dark side.

Brontë chooses the relentless desolation and isolation of the Yorkshire moors as her setting, which is where she grew up. Not only is the landscape thematic—a dark and dramatic setting for dark and dramatic people—it also creates a closed-room situation that allows her to keep a sharp focus on the characters populating the two estates: Wuthering Heights and Thrushcross Grange. You'd think the limited number of characters would make them easy to follow, but you'd be wrong. Everyone marries their cousin, and both first and last names play musical chairs.

But Brontë has done this for a reason. The generational aspect of the novel is important—how one is raised and what gets passed on form the thematic foundation of the book. The generations also form the two halves of the narrative structure. And the one character we never lose sight of is the one who has only a single name: Heathcliff. He is never given a family name, which becomes ironic considering his narrative goal is to inherit the family's fortune and estate.

Heathcliff is an antihero and is the chief protagonist in the novel. But because the story is narrated primarily by two other characters (Mr. Lockwood and Nelly Dean), the structural elements become a little… confusing. As well, both Catherine (the elder) and Cathy (the younger) play key roles—the latter eventually redeeming the behavior of the former and becoming a secondary protagonist.

Narrative Goal

Heathcliff's story forms the backbone of the novel:

When Heathcliff is adopted by the Earnshaws, he forms a passionate bond with Catherine. But when Hindley humiliates him and obstructs his love for Catherine, Heathcliff vows a revenge of disinheritance and ruin that spans generations. Ultimately, he must find a way to overcome his hatred and bitterness if he ever wants to attain peace in a reunion with Catherine after death.

The Frame

The novel opens just before the climax. Mr. Lockwood is not a protagonist, but he kicks off the narration (and his presence actually provokes the climax). His meeting with the inhabitants of Wuthering Heights is what leads Nelly Dean, the true narrator, to tell her story.

It is 1801 when Mr. Lockwood comes to Wuthering Heights to meet his landlord, Heathcliff. Lockwood is the new tenant at Thrushcross Grange, four miles away. While this meeting inspires some curiosity on Lockwood's part, his kickstarting of the climax happens on a subsequent visit when he gets stuck at Wuthering Heights due to a snowstorm and must spend the night. He ends up staying in a small room where the name Catherine is written all over the walls. He finds Catherine's diary and reads an entry. That night he has a nightmare in which he sees a girl trying to get in through the room's window. She identifies herself as Catherine Linton.

Heathcliff's reaction to this news—deep emotion and heartrending grief—is a turning point that eventually leads him into his final transformation. But in terms of the narrative frame, this moment is also what pushes Lockwood to ask the housekeeper Nelly Dean if she knows the story behind the inhabitants of Wuthering Heights.

PLOT POINTS

Stasis

We shift back to 1767, when the Earnshaw family lived at Wuthering Heights: Catherine, her brother Hindley, and their parents. One day, Mr. Earnshaw goes to Liverpool and returns with a desperate-looking young orphan they name Heathcliff. This is the early catalyst. Without this event, there would be no story, but we're still a long way from the inciting incident where Heathcliff's narrative goal forms.

Mr. Earnshaw develops a particular fondness for Heathcliff and soon prefers him to his son Hindley. This sets up a rivalry that will endure throughout the novel. But for now, Hindley is sent away to school. While he's gone, Heathcliff and Catherine develop an extremely close relationship that renders them soulmates. They're both wild, partners in crime, always getting into trouble. This becomes a passion that never leaves Heathcliff and that he will make everyone pay for when it is thwarted (and, in a real sense, stolen from him).

Three years later, when Mr. Earnshaw dies, the estate of Wuthering Heights passes on to Hindley. Hindley returns with a wife, takes control of the house, and becomes tyrannical, determined to split up Heathcliff and Catherine as retribution for his father's preference of Heathcliff as a son. This introduces both hatred and vengeance into the household, inheritances that are passed on as easily as wealth. But we are still in stasis mode here.

Inciting Incident

The inciting incident begins when Heathcliff and Catherine are out on the moors and end up at Thrushcross Grange, where they spy on the well-mannered and well-to-do children Edgar and Isabella Linton. When Catherine gets bitten by their dog, the parents insist she stay there to convalesce. They won't let Heathcliff into the house because he looks too wild, so he returns to Wuthering Heights, where he is severely neglected by Hindley.

When Catherine returns home five weeks later, she has been transformed into a refined young woman. She's well-dressed, clean, and polite—in huge contrast to Heathcliff, whom Hindley has treated like a servant and who hasn't washed in weeks. Catherine still cares for Heathcliff, but her treatment of him changes. She sees him through new eyes, evaluates him as inferior, wonders why he's so dirty and rude.

Heathcliff internalizes this feeling of inferiority. He is the orphan, the one who doesn't belong. Hindley's poor treatment of him accomplishes his goal of damaging the relationship between Heathcliff and Catherine. When the Lintons visit and Hindley orders Heathcliff to remain in the garret, out of sight, a fight ensues, and Heathcliff is further humiliated. This is when his narrative goal is formed, which he declares to Nelly: "I'm trying to settle how I shall pay Hindley back. I don't care how long I wait, if I can only do it at last."

Point of No Return

Having spent so much time with the Lintons, Catherine develops a fondness for Edgar (or, in truth, for Edgar's money and social position). She confides to Nelly that Edgar has proposed and she has accepted.

Unbeknownst to Catherine, Heathcliff is in the room. What Heathcliff hears her say is that it would degrade her to marry him the way he is now, having been ruined by Hindley. What he does not hear her say (because he sneaks out of the room in humiliation) is how much she loves Heathcliff, that she *is* Heathcliff. He runs away, and when Catherine realizes why, she searches the moors for him and becomes dangerously ill.

That night—the night Heathcliff and Catherine are separated—a tree splits in a storm. Nerd alert: this is an interesting crossover with *Jane Eyre*, written by Emily Brontë's sister Charlotte, wherein a tree splits in a storm when Jane and Mr. Rochester are separated. (A tree must have split in a storm in the authors' real lives. We can imagine a dinnertime conversation in which the sisters argue over who gets to use the tree in their novel.)

Rising Action

When Hindley's wife dies of consumption after giving birth to a son (Hareton), Hindley goes off the rails, drinking and gambling, never to regain his footing. But that is not enough of a failure to satisfy Heathcliff. Indeed, it's just the beginning.

Catherine survives her illness and marries Edgar, and Nelly goes to live with them, leaving five-year-old Hareton to his fate with a negligent father.

Three years after Heathcliff disappears, he shows up again at Thrushcross Grange, unrecognizable. He has money now, and an education—the very things he was lacking when Catherine said it would degrade her to marry him. It's clear that his bond with Catherine has survived. They pick up where they left off, much to Edgar's concern. While Heathcliff goes to live at Wuthering Heights with Hindley and Hareton, he also spends a lot of time at the Grange with Catherine.

But it soon becomes apparent there's another reason he's staying at Wuthering Heights. When Nelly goes to visit, the child, Hareton, is violent and illiterate. He curses her. She assumes Hindley has raised the boy to be like this, but she discovers it's Heathcliff who's ruining him—and meanwhile also encouraging Hindley to gamble and mortgage away the Heights... to him.

Heathcliff has come back with a two-part plan that he now sets in motion. He is a man who was wronged and mistreated, and he's returned to wreak that mistreatment on whomever he can. Hareton is not the only victim. Isabella Linton, who lives with Edgar and Catherine at the Grange, has fallen in love with Heathcliff. But Heathcliff couldn't care less about her—because the second part of his plan is that he wants Catherine back.

When Edgar and Heathcliff have a falling out, Edgar insists that Catherine must choose between Heathcliff and him. Never one to take kindly to being told what to do, Catherine locks herself in her room and goes on a hunger strike. Meanwhile, Edgar warns Isabella that if she marries Heathcliff, he will cut her off financially and won't have anything more to do with her.

In the melee of Catherine getting dangerously sick, Isabella runs off with Heathcliff. We then get her POV from a letter Nelly receives, letting us in on the state of things at Wuthering Heights. Hindley is a disaster. He's a drunk, and his gambling has ruined him financially. Basically, he has traded circumstances with Heathcliff. Hareton is being raised without any manners or the ability to read or write (another trade in circumstances with Heathcliff). The house is a mess. And Isabella deeply regrets her marriage. But her brother refuses to intervene, so she eventually runs away to London where she gives birth to Heathcliff's son, the sickly Linton.

Midpoint

At the midpoint of the novel, the focus shifts from the older characters (Catherine, Hindley, Edgar, and Isabella) to the younger ones (Hareton, Cathy, and Linton)—with the one constant being Heathcliff. The older characters wronged Heathcliff, and he in turn intends to avenge himself on the younger ones.

The arc of the first half of the novel ends in despair with the death of Catherine after she gives birth to a child named (you guessed it) Catherine (though everyone refers to her as Cathy). Before she dies, Heathcliff begs her to haunt him, but she doesn't, and he becomes even more of a misery to be around.

Isabella Linton dies as well, but by that time Linton Heathcliff is twelve years old (and still sickly). Linton lives for a time with Edgar and Nelly, but then Heathcliff arrives at Thrushcross Grange to claim him as his son and to raise (i.e., ruin) him.

Nelly and Edgar do everything they can to keep young Cathy away from Wuthering Heights, but one day when she is thirteen, she wanders away on her pony and ends up there, only to discover she has two cousins: Linton and Hareton. As Cathy can be considered a secondary protagonist, this is the inciting incident of her storyline (and her "meet-cute" moment).

By then, Hareton is eighteen, strong, good-looking, and completely illiterate, which Cathy ridicules him for. Linton is younger than Cathy and is whiny and needy, but at least he's not an imbecile. There is an interesting generational parallel here. While Cathy ridicules Hareton, there is a subtext of attraction between them that mirrors the attraction between Catherine and Heathcliff. Cathy should never marry Linton—just like Catherine should never have married Edgar.

But in keeping with Heathcliff's plan to ruin everyone and inherit everything, Cathy and Linton must marry. This is the final obstacle in the achievement of his goal. Hindley dies, having mortgaged Wuthering Heights to Heathcliff, but he is still not the legal heir of Thrushcross Grange. He counts on Linton dying young—which is certain to happen, given how sickly he is. To that end, Heathcliff does everything possible to get Linton and Cathy together.

When Cathy next comes to visit at Wuthering Heights, Hareton has learned to read his own name. He's quite proud of this, but she still belittles him. Hareton reacts with anger, and we can't help but feel sorry for him. The message—that so much of what we become is the result of how we've been treated (or mistreated)—was a pretty revolutionary insight at the time.

All Is Lost—For Both Heathcliff and Cathy

When Cathy and Nelly come to Wuthering Heights while Cathy's father, Edgar, is on his deathbed, Heathcliff locks them up until Cathy agrees to marry Linton. Linton manages to get Cathy out so she can see her father before he dies. But they do marry, thus denying Hareton his relationship with Cathy.

Linton dies soon after, as expected, and it seems Heathcliff has achieved his goal at last: he is the master of both Wuthering Heights and Thrushcross Grange. Everyone around him is either dead or desperately unhappy. So, is he overwhelmed with the joy of his victory? Not quite. Too often, what we want is not what we need.

The story could end here, but it doesn't, because it turns out Heathcliff achieving his goal of revenge is precisely what stands in the way of his ultimate goal, which is to be reunited in some manner with his true love, Catherine. Her ghost still won't come to him. For this to happen, he must let go of his bitterness and hatred. In short, he must allow the second generation to achieve what the first could not and let the love between Cathy and Hareton flourish.

Climax—and the Return of Lockwood's Narration

When Lockwood returns six months later, there are great changes all around, and Nelly fills him (and us) in. Nelly now lives at Wuthering Heights. Heathcliff has died. And Cathy and Hareton are in love and plan to be married. This shift is key in the redemption of the ending and the reversal of what happened between Catherine and Heathcliff.

Nelly explains how it came about. After Linton dies, Cathy begins to feel bad for having teased Hareton and helps him learn how to read. She apologizes to him, and he forgives her. Their affection for each other grows into a force powerful enough to offset Heathcliff's bitterness. Thus, Cathy achieves her narrative goal.

Some critics claim it is Heathcliff's death that allows Cathy and Hareton's love to flourish. While it may be true that Cathy and Hareton could not have gotten engaged if Heathcliff was alive, it's the fulfillment of their love that finally releases Heathcliff. After their love blooms, Catherine's spirit comes to Heathcliff, thus suggesting that his vengeance and hatred blocked it all along. It is implied that Heathcliff comes to realize this after Lockwood (in the beginning) tells him about his ghostly vision in Catherine's bedroom.

Resolution

In the resolution of the novel, Heathcliff spends several sleepless nights wandering the moors and finally dies—in a state of ecstasy—in the tiny room where Lockwood once spent the night.

Cathy and Hareton plan to be married; Catherine and Heathcliff are together after death. Love proves itself more powerful than hatred. A mostly tragic story ends with redemption.

A Masterpiece of Narration

The novel's structure is complicated by the layers of narration that give us two timelines. The present moment story is mostly narrated by Mr. Lockwood, Heathcliff's new tenant at Thrushcross Grange. It takes place in 1801–1802 and neatly bookends the novel. The past that spans the thirty or so years previous makes up the bulk of the story and is largely narrated by Nelly Dean, the housekeeper (though technically it is Lockwood who records it in his diary). There are occasional dips into the present to remind us that this is a told story, and there are dips from present into past to fill in the blanks that Lockwood couldn't possibly have discovered himself. The result is a masterpiece of narration that is an accomplishment in itself.

Mr. Lockwood, the initial narrator, is more of a plot construct than anything, and as such is the least dynamic of the characters. He's sort of a stand-in for the reader, functioning more as a listener than an active force. He enters the story on the same footing we do, as a stranger to Wuthering Heights, unsure of what he's seeing. His visits allow us before and after pictures of the Heights—namely, before and after forgiveness and the redemptive power of love, the only things capable of triumphing over Heathcliff's enduring hatred and desire for vengeance. It is only thanks to the triumph of love that Heathcliff is finally released from hatred and able to die and be with his true love, Catherine.

Nelly Dean is the chief narrator, having been the housekeeper at Wuthering Heights when Catherine and her brother Hindley were young and Heathcliff first arrived. The narration occasionally passes to other characters and takes other forms: entries from Catherine's diary, a letter from Isabella Linton, and brief moments from Heathcliff himself and another servant at the Heights named Zillah.

It's Nelly who fills in the history for Mr. Lockwood after he's been to Wuthering Heights a few times and is confounded by its gloomy atmosphere and hostile inhabitants. It was common in gothic novels to employ a narrator like Nelly who is not directly involved in the story. The idea is that the subjective and unreliable narration would contribute to the eerie atmosphere and create more mystery and ambiguity. On that level, it succeeds. We can never be entirely certain that what she's telling Lockwood is true. Nelly is judgmental and has her own strong opinions that color how she tells the story and what she chooses to relate. She also harbors some bitterness toward Heathcliff. She wants to be allowed to stay at Wuthering Heights when Cathy marries Linton, but Heathcliff won't allow it.

Nelly paints Heathcliff as an almost cartoonish villain. And there is no denying he's a hard man—violent, abusive, and mean. But when we see the way Cathy ridicules Hareton for faults he cannot help, given his upbringing, we are reminded that Heathcliff was legitimately wronged in this story. It's also worth remembering that Heathcliff is capable of love. Most of what he's done as an adult has come from an attempt to better himself and make himself worthy in Catherine's eyes.

Things Happen in Twos

Duality is an interesting feature of *Wuthering Heights*. There are two estates, two generations of characters, two timelines, two main narrators—and one Heathcliff. What's interesting about this is that Heathcliff contains two opposing potentials: he's smart and attractive and capable of great love. But after being humiliated and wronged, he is also capable of turning his intelligence toward vengeance and hatred. He is both protagonist and antagonist. Given a different set of circumstances, he would have become a completely different person.

The Catherine/Cathy parallel allows for a redemptive turn in the story. What went wrong in the first generation gets corrected in the second.

Why Is *Wuthering Heights* a Classic?

Some readers contend it's the frankness that Brontë used to create characters who all possess a dark side that makes this novel a classic. It may also be one of the first novels to demonstrate the devastating cyclical nature of abuse: the claustrophobic imprisonment of family, the power of nurture over nature, and how nurture (or its lack) can have such a terrible effect—and ultimately that the lack of nurture can be redeemed. Indeed, the novel's portrayal of domestic abuse made it controversial when it was first published.

But we would contend it's Brontë's layers of narration and the essential unreliability of her narrators that make this book so interesting and re-readable. Heathcliff is an antihero—not the first one in literature, but pretty much an archetype by now. Every character gives the reader a reason not to like them, and yet we are still willing to follow them to the end.

Chapter Summary: Moor than a Feeling

Emily Brontë's *Wuthering Heights* is a great novel to analyze for its complex narrative structure and its antihero. The echoing of plot points in this generational diptych lifts the novel out of tragedy and allows for a certain amount of redemption. As Flaubert does in

Madame Bovary, Brontë proves with the character of Heathcliff that a protagonist doesn't have to be likable for readers to follow them; they just have to be interesting.

Elements of the Gothic Novel: When it comes to the typical elements in a gothic novel, *Wuthering Heights* checks most of the boxes.

- A menacing setting: the Yorkshire moors
- Romance: Heathcliff's passion for Catherine
- Elements of the supernatural: Catherine's hauntings
- Intense emotions: everyone seems to suffer from this
- An antihero: Heathcliff
- Female victims: pretty much every female character in the novel becomes one
- Visions and nightmares: Lockwood has one, then Heathcliff has more later
- Madness: Hindley can be said to suffer from it after his wife dies
- Gloomy weather: this seems present for most of the year

The only thing missing are prophecies and curses, but then again, there's Joseph, the cantankerous servant who's always either quoting scripture or cursing someone. He speaks in such a heavy Yorkshire dialect it's almost impossible to understand him, though that doesn't seem to matter. It's hard to imagine a character more miserable than Heathcliff, but Joseph wins that award.

Antihero: An antihero is a central character who lacks conventional heroic attributes traditionally associated with protagonists. Unlike classic heroes, who exhibit qualities such as bravery, morality, and idealism, antiheroes are flawed individuals with traits that might be considered villainous, such as dishonesty, aggression, or a lack of morality. They may be driven by self-interest, revenge, or personal desires rather than altruistic goals.

The antihero's appeal lies in their complexity and relatability. They often grapple with internal conflicts, moral ambiguities, and a troubled past, which adds depth to their character. This complexity often leads to themes of redemption, the duality of human nature, and the blurred lines between good and evil.

In addition to Heathcliff, classic examples include Jay Gatsby in *The Great Gatsby*, whose pursuit of the American Dream is tainted by corruption; Dorian Gray in *The Picture of Dorian Gray*, who is consumed by vanity and moral decay; and Fred Vincy in *Middlemarch*, whose laziness and irresponsibility hinder his growth until he confronts his flaws.

Brideshead Revisited

by Evelyn Waugh

Amazing Grace?

In December 1943, Evelyn Waugh had a parachuting accident and was laid up for six months on "soya beans and Basic English." What does an author do in those circumstances? Write a novel about the age of nobility, of course, and fill it with all the decadent meals they're missing. Years later, Waugh found such details distasteful, but the novel still makes top 100 lists of best work in world literature.

According to Waugh, a convert to Catholicism, this is a book about grace. In 1967, literary critic Roland Barthes wrote an essay in which he argued that just because an author claims that the novel they wrote means X doesn't mean we have to believe it means X. We held on to that notion for a while as we thought about this novel, but in the end, the structure didn't make sense until we embraced Waugh's intentions.

Waugh wrote *Brideshead Revisited* in the middle of World War Two, in Europe, when death and destruction were everywhere and there was no end in sight. The motif of empty houses, the elegiac tone of loss, the notion that life doesn't end up the way we expect and things tend to go to shit—it's no wonder he reaches for grace as an answer. In a religious worldview, human beings will always let us down. God does not.

A Structural Venn Diagram

The protagonist, Charles Ryder, states: "My theme is memory, that winged host that soared about me one grey morning of war-time." This would have been an especially powerful theme in the early 1940s in Europe. The desire for the idyllic parts of our lives to never end. For people not to turn into alcoholics and marriages not to end in divorce. For peacetime not to descend into war. It's no accident that Charles becomes an artist—and that his subject is houses slated for destruction. Not only is this a way of preserving the past, but it's also his way of making time stand still.

But that is just the theme. What Charles seeks is love. He states his goal clearly early in the book, and when he meets Sebastian, he believes he has achieved it. All he has to do now is hold on to it.

That turns out to be easier said than done. Charles thinks he wants the love of Sebastian, but this is a fundamentally religious novel. No human being will ever satisfy the need for true love, which is divine. When Charles' relationship with Sebastian fails, as it is destined to do, he looks for substitutes to replicate it—art, and then Sebastian's sister Julia. But he cannot get what he wants, no matter how many ways he tries. He can only get what he needs, which is the love of God. Waugh calls it grace, the "twitch upon the thread." After a lifetime of agnosticism, Charles ends up on his knees in prayer.

The story is bookended by a prologue and epilogue, thus employing a frame narrative with three sections in the middle. Each of Charles' four storylines centers on an attempt at love: his love of Sebastian, his love of art, his love of Julia, and his eventual love of God. But these arcs are not self-contained. They overlap each other much like a series of Venn diagrams, and they all exist within the larger spiritual context.

To put the main structure and narrative goal into its simplest form: When Charles Ryder falls in love with Sebastian, he believes he has entered Eden and wants nothing more than to remain there. But Sebastian is human and therefore flawed. When temptation arrives in the form of alcoholism, Charles loses Sebastian. He tries to regain that love first by becoming an artist and then through his relationship with Julia, but he's (yes, we're going to say it) looking for love in all the wrong places, and both attempts end in failure. True love can only be achieved through the love of God, and unless Charles finds it, he will remain a cynical and unhappy man.

PLOT POINTS

Beginning with the All-Is-Lost Moment

The novel opens with a prologue set in the 1940s. Captain Charles Ryder is an army officer, and the Marchmain family is firmly in the rearview mirror of his life. At thirty-nine, Charles has grown disillusioned with his army position—and really, with his life. World War Two is dragging on. The company is stationed next to an asylum, and the joke is that everyone in there seems happier than they are in the army. When a transfer comes, the soldiers expect to see action in the Middle East, but this is just another in a series of random transfers to somewhere in rural England.

But for Charles it turns out to be grace in action. And Charles is someone who has not believed in grace his entire life.

The company arrives at their new headquarters in the dark, so Charles is unaware of where they are. As soon as he hears the name Brideshead, memories flood in of this grand home and the family who owns it: the Marchmains. As in Proust's *In Search of Lost Time*, when Marcel dips his madeleine into the tea, this is the catalyst for Charles to tell his story. In the chronology of the story itself, however, we are at the all-is-lost moment, on the edge of his climax.

Love #1: Sebastian
Stasis and Inciting Incident

Sebastian Flyte represents Charles' first attempt to find love in the fallible human world. The story shifts back over twenty years, to when Charles first saw Brideshead Castle. He was with Sebastian, whom he'd met at Oxford. We flash further back to the stasis of this first story arc, when Charles receives advice from his cousin never to take ground-floor rooms at Oxford. But had he not taken a ground-floor room, he would never have met Sebastian.

At the time, it seems funny that Sebastian wanders drunk into Charles' flat while he's having a party and throws up in the middle of it. That's their meet-cute moment, and it's the inciting incident of this arc. But as the story proceeds, it will become uncomfortably prophetic.

The narrative in this section centers on Charles' time at Oxford, his relationship with Sebastian—and Sebastian's descent into alcoholism, which at this point still falls on the side of casual drinking. While Waugh never states that this is a homosexual relationship (unlike with Sebastian's friend Anthony Blanche, who is openly gay), it seems clear that it is. Charles is "in search of love," and when he meets Sebastian, it's like finding "that low door in the wall… which opened on an enclosed and enchanted garden."

Charles thinks he has entered an Eden-like garden. He thinks he's found true love with Sebastian, but Sebastian (like all humans) is destined to let him down because… *Et in Arcadia Ego*. The phrase is written on a skull Charles buys and places in a bowl of roses. *Death exists even in paradise*—but Charles doesn't see this yet. He is bewitched by Sebastian and by the idea that Sebastian can fulfill his need. He doesn't see that this need is spiritual—and how could he? He's a staunch agnostic. Even when surrounded by the Catholic Marchmains, he refuses to embrace faith.

Rising Action

Sebastian and Charles go to Brideshead and meet Nanny, but Sebastian doesn't want Charles to meet his family.

Though many of the Marchmains are devout Catholics, they are far from perfect. Lord Marchmain lives in Venice with another woman and has rejected his faith. Lady Marchmain won't grant him a divorce. She is described as a saint but is pushy and evangelistic. Brideshead (Bridey), the eldest son, is a gloomy rule-bound Catholic. Julia wrestles with her faith in a materialistic and superficial world. Only Cordelia (age ten) has a true spirit of joy.

When Sebastian breaks his ankle and calls Charles down to Brideshead Castle to keep him from getting bored, the two other love arcs are introduced as catalysts: Julia, who resembles Sebastian physically but not emotionally (she's more mature); and art. When Julia picks up Charles at the train station, there's a spark of attraction between them, but she doesn't stay. Sebastian, who has brought beauty into Charles' world, encourages his artistic talent, and Charles begins to paint. Both these threads—Julia and art—will become arcs in their own right as substitutes for Sebastian after he fades from Charles' life.

Sebastian takes Charles to Venice to meet his father, who is "living in sin," and Lord Marchmain's girlfriend warns Charles that Sebastian is childish and drinks too much—and in a dangerous way. It's another prophetic moment.

Midpoint

Charles and Sebastian return to Oxford for another term, but things have changed. Charles begins a serious study of art. Sebastian, however, remains in party mode. He drives drunk, and he, Charles, and another friend are arrested. They wrangle a reduced sentence thanks to the intervention of Julia's boyfriend Rex, but this is the beginning of the downward slide for Sebastian. While Charles takes a step toward maturity, Sebastian starts drinking more seriously, and alone.

Rising Action

Charles decides to leave Oxford to pursue his passion for painting. In an effort to control Sebastian, Lady Marchmain enlists Mr. Samgrass, a history don, to take him on a tour of orthodox monasteries, but the trip is a disaster. Sebastian sneaks away and gallivants around Europe with Anthony Blanche. After Christmas, when Charles comes to visit Brideshead, the mood in the house is tense and there is a marked reduction in the availability of alcohol. Lady Marchmain is in damage-control mode, but Sebastian finds ways to get alcohol and drinks in secret.

False Victory

When Sebastian declares he will join Cordelia and Bridey to go hunting, everyone jumps on it as a victory. But Sebastian is already beyond hope, and Lady Marchmain's pushiness backfires. Sebastian asks Charles to give him money, and he relents, thus aiding in his fall. The day ends disastrously. Sebastian ends up getting hammered.

Tragic Climax

Sebastian tells Charles to leave Brideshead. The low door in the wall shuts. Charles has been kicked out of Eden. In an attempt to hold on to love in some form, he moves to Paris to study art.

Resolution

At Lady Marchmain's request on her deathbed, Charles tracks down Sebastian. He is in Morocco drinking his life away with a down-and-out German from the Foreign Legion named Kurt. There's no doubt Kurt is taking advantage of him, but Sebastian enjoys caring for him and refuses to return to England. His relationship with Charles is officially over.

Love #2: Art

Catalyst and Inciting Incident

Because there are overlaps between these storylines, the first few structural elements of the art arc have already been planted. The catalyst was Sebastian's introduction of beauty into Charles' life, and the inciting incident was his encouragement of Charles' talent.

Rising Action

As mentioned, Charles becomes more serious about his studies and realizes he's wasting his time at Oxford. If he wants to become an artist, he must go to Paris, which is what he does after his relationship with Sebastian falls apart.

Midpoint

Lord Marchmain's debts are so onerous he must sell the London home. Since it's slated for destruction, Bridey hires Charles to paint four paintings so that they can remember it. This commission seals Charles' vocation as an architectural painter, particularly of structures in decline. Not only does his vocation strike an elegiac tone, but there is also a wonderful spiritual symbolism of the impermanence of man-made structures.

Rising Action

Ten years go by. Charles finds success as an artist specializing in painting pictures of condemned buildings. He spends two years on his own in Latin America painting abandoned structures that have been overcome by nature. His marriage to a woman named Celia is loveless. He only married her because he misses Sebastian. He has two children, one of whom he's never met, and neither of whom he appears to care for. Whatever love he has for art, it doesn't spill over into his human relationships.

False Victory

At the exhibition of his Latin American paintings in London, Charles hears that the critics who once criticized his work now call it "virile." Things are looking up.

Tragic Climax

Anthony Blanche shows up unexpectedly at the exhibition and suggests that Charles' work is essentially crap. "English charm" is what he calls it—meaning it's superficial. The love Charles thought he found as a substitute for Sebastian is nothing but a sham.

Resolution

Charles has been using art to hide from political reality, but he accepts that war is on the horizon and signs up to aid the war effort.

Love #3: Julia

Catalyst and Inciting Incident

This arc also has a lot of overlap with the art arc. As mentioned, Charles met Julia long ago (the catalyst) and was attracted to her, particularly as she physically resembles Sebastian. She marries Rex, a non-Catholic, a cynic, and a politician—and the marriage is a disaster.

On his way back from Latin America, Charles meets up with his wife Celia in New York, and they take the ship back to England together. It turns out Julia and Rex are also on the boat. A storm erupts (the inciting incident), and most people on the boat are seasick, but Charles and Julia are not—which means they spend lots of time together.

Rising Action

Charles and Julia sleep together on the ship. When they arrive in London, Charles stays on without Celia—ostensibly for the exhibition of his artwork but also so that he can spend time with Julia. Celia figures out Charles is cheating on her, but she has also cheated on him, so the breakdown of their marriage is expected.

Julia's situation is complicated by her religion. She believes her poor marriage is a punishment for marrying outside the Church, and she only capitulates to adultery because she assumes she is beyond saving.

Midpoint

After two years, she and Charles are still together but haven't married because neither is divorced yet. Julia wants to get married because war is coming, but when Bridey describes her relationship with Charles as "living in sin," she gets upset. Her guilt is accruing. Charles says religion is foolish, but she realizes she doesn't want to turn her back on God anymore.

Rising Action

Lord Marchmain arrives from Venice very ill, wanting to spend his last days at Brideshead. Cordelia arrives with news of Sebastian, and Julia is concerned that Charles has forgotten him. Charles calls Sebastian "the forerunner" to Julia. She says, "...perhaps I am only a forerunner, too." In a key moment, Charles says, "...perhaps all our loves are merely hints and symbols." Humans are bound to be disappointed in their search for love because the thing they're really looking for is "always a pace or two ahead of us."

False Victory

Cordelia represents the voice of spiritual, unconditional love, and as she speaks to Charles about their love for Sebastian, he *almost* gets it—glimpsing a love that goes beyond typical romance.

Tragic Climax

As Lord Marchmain nears death, Bridey wants to call a priest to deliver the last rites, even though Lord Marchmain has rejected Catholicism most of his life. Charles is appalled, calling the priest a witch doctor and religion mumbo-jumbo—which causes an argument between him and Julia. Sure enough, when the priest arrives the first time, Lord Marchmain orders him out. But the second time he comes, Charles prays for God to forgive Lord Marchmain's sins—if only for Julia's sake. Lord Marchmain finally makes a sign of the cross and is saved. His salvation seals Julia's decision: she cannot marry Charles. The marriage would put her too far away from God.

Resolution

Both Julia and Charles sign up to help the war effort. They do not marry. Charles joins the army, entering the lowest (and most loveless) part of his life. That leads us into the prologue/epilogue where we began—but not where we'll end.

Love #4: God

Inciting Incident

Charles' love of Sebastian introduces him to paradise, the Garden of Eden, but it cannot last.

Rising Action

Charles meets the Marchmain family, each a representative of a different way of being Catholic, but he remains insistent on his agnosticism.

The relationship between Charles and Sebastian breaks down, signifying the Fall. The door to the garden slams shut. Charles must navigate the real world, where Sebastian is an alcoholic, Lady Marchmain dies, and Lord Marchmain is in debt. All he can do is turn to art.

Midpoint

With Julia, Charles realizes that perhaps all human love is merely a hint of something greater.

Rising Action

Cordelia talks about grace, quoting a line from a G.K. Chesterton novel that describes how anyone can be brought back to God no matter how far they've strayed. All He has to do is give a twitch on the thread. Nevertheless, Charles fights the idea of a priest coming to give last rites to Lord Marchmain, but he prays for Julia's sake, and when Lord Marchmain makes the sign of the cross, "the veil of the temple [is] rent from top to bottom."

Climax

Back in Brideshead as an army officer, Charles visits the chapel, which has been reopened because of the army's presence there, and prays. He finds a small lamp, still lit—a symbol of hope in a dark world.

Resolution

Charles comes away from the moment with a new feeling of happiness—having finally found what he's been looking for all along.

The Motif of Home

Home is one of the key motifs of the novel. The prologue presents us with the asylum, an appropriate choice in the middle of war. Nothing that's happening around Charles makes sense. The company is moved for no apparent reason, jobs are assigned that aren't important. War is inherently nuts.

Book One of the novel centers on Brideshead Castle, an enchanted place. When Charles speaks of the low door in the wall, it's not only Sebastian who is the enchanted garden behind it; it's also Brideshead. This is the Garden of Eden, and Brideshead is paradise. For a while.

Book Two moves the reader to the Marchmains' London home. This is the Fall, when everything is in decline. Charles loses Sebastian and embraces his vocation as a painter of architecture—homes that are set to be destroyed.

In Book Three, there is a sense of homelessness. Much of this section takes place in a storm on board a ship, and then with all the various marriages, divorces, and deaths, the notion of a stable home becomes uncertain. The essence of life is change. The movement of the ocean is echoed by movement on land. Everyone is changing houses.

Charles has a dream about a home destroyed by avalanche, which points to the parable of building a house on a strong foundation. Because Charles has *built his house* on human love, it is destined to fail. In the end, when Lord Marchmain, who rejected Catholicism, returns to the fold upon his death, it seems Waugh is suggesting another home: heaven.

The epilogue takes us back to wartime. Brideshead has been transformed into barracks. But this time, the building that becomes the focus is the reopened chapel, a place Charles ignored during his earlier time at Brideshead.

Why Is *Brideshead Revisited* a Classic?

Aside from an impressively complex structure, Waugh presents us with strong memorable characters and a theme that is disconcertingly relatable: how to stop time from passing, how to stop life from changing—and how to find love. Is faith possible in a superficial world? Is hope possible? These are questions we will continue to ask. *Brideshead Revisited* provides us with one possible answer.

Chapter Summary: Grace Expectations

Brideshead Revisited is a masterful juggling of arcs, each overlapping with the one that follows, all of them building to a climax. Waugh utilizes both narrative goals and motifs to create thematic cohesion in the novel. He also employs the want-versus-need dichotomy to push his protagonist through to the end.

Motifs: A motif is a recurring element—such as an image, symbol, phrase, or concept—that appears throughout a literary work and holds significant meaning. Motifs are used to reinforce and develop the themes of the narrative. Themes, on the other hand, are the central ideas or messages explored in a literary work. They are the overarching topics or questions that the narrative seeks to examine, such as love, identity, or the passage of time.

While motifs and themes are interconnected, motifs are the tangible or perceptible elements that recur and point toward the larger, more abstract themes. Motifs act as threads weaving through the narrative, connecting various parts of the story and highlighting the thematic concerns.

So What?: Theme asks the question: *So what? What is this book about? Why am I reading this?* Usually, the theme in a novel seems so intentional that it must have been planned out from the start, but that's not necessarily the case. Often, in writing a novel, the theme doesn't become apparent until after one or two complete drafts—and even then, it's not always easy for the author to realize what they've done. Sometimes it takes an objective pair of eyes to tease out the thematic threads.

A theme might be a statement. It might also be a dilemma for the reader to ponder. When you're not sure what the theme of a novel is, look at the protagonist. What do they learn? What do they have to figure out over the course of the story? That will be the theme. When we look at Charles Ryder and his attempts to find love in all the wrong places, the theme of grace becomes obvious.

The Glue: Both themes and motifs create cohesion in a novel, bringing all the disparate pieces together. The motif of homes appears in every book of *Brideshead Revisited* and helps to solidify the novel, as does Charles' search for love that culminates in grace.

In Conclusion

Studying the work of the masters is an excellent way to get a handle on narrative structure. At a glance, the traditional plot points we've discussed might seem formulaic, but when it comes to wildly successful and widely adored novels, these traditional structures are nearly universal.

In case you're thinking, *well, that's fine for authors who were writing a hundred years ago, but how will studying these novels help me in my writing right now? Hasn't structure changed since then?*

It's true that some tastes have changed. Most contemporary authors choose first person or deep third over the traditional omniscient narrator found in many classics because that's what readers today prefer. But storytelling itself? It might surprise you to discover that no, it hasn't really changed. Why? Because narrative structure is connected to reader psychology—our need to immerse ourselves in the fictional world, to anticipate (or dread) what will happen next, to empathize with and/or identify with the protagonist.

Studying the strategies and techniques employed by these classic authors will give you more tools in your writers' toolbox and afford you some different approaches to your material. We hope these works inspire you to get creative with the structure of your novel—the caveat being: as long as it serves the story. That is the key. If structural pyrotechnics don't serve the story you're telling, they will come across as gimmicky and contrived. But if they do serve it, you might create a novel that readers a hundred years from now will be talking about and dissecting in essays and lecture halls, wondering how you did it.

Answer? The story had good bones.

Thank You for Reading!

If you enjoyed *Story Skeleton: The Classics*, we would love it if you left a review on either Amazon or Goodreads. Reviews are incredibly important—they help other writers discover the book and support us as authors.

We also welcome your feedback: editors@darlingaxe.com

Your support means the world to us. Thank you!

Bonus Chapter from
Immersion and Emotion: The Two Pillars of Storytelling
The Heart of Fiction

When a novel captures you, you turn pages obsessively to find out what will happen next. This might seem like an interest in the plot, but that obsession actually stems from a strong connection with the main character. The author has made you care. You're invested in the outcome. Sometimes you even feel like these are real people you're reading about. *I know that person*, you think. Or even—*the author is writing about me*.

Character is at the heart of all fiction, regardless of the genre. When you're reading a book and you discover you don't care what happens in the end, it's not a failure of plot: it's a failure of character. The novel is peopled by cardboard or stereotypical figures. They don't live on the page.

So, how do you give your character a heartbeat?

The Character Questionnaire

These long lists of character questions that exist on the internet are great for fleshing out the details of your character, but they won't work the magic we're talking about here. They will only (or mostly) provide external details—her favorite shirt, his preferred nickname, the object they can't part with. Those are all interesting, but they're not what bring a character to life.

The heart of a character is internal conflict, which is woven into external conflict, which is woven into goals and theme and plot. Surprise: it's all connected. A novel should be a house of cards—pull one card, and it all threatens to collapse. Why? Because it functions as a cohesive whole. It must. When it doesn't, you've got a fractured, anecdotal mess on your hands, with characters doing things that don't make sense or fit with the narrative.

Internal Conflict and a Weird Pair of Glasses

The external conflict in a novel is the plot—it's what happens from inciting incident to climax. But the protagonist is the engine that drives that plot forward. They act. They act on purpose because they want something. Desperately. For the entire novel, they're trying to get what they want. Everything in the novel is caused by their attempts to achieve that goal.

However, our most powerful desires are not random. When we want something desperately, there's a strong *why* attached to our goal. That *why* is what makes readers care. It's what makes the story matter. Without it, it's just a car chase for no reason.

But here's the catch. We often want the wrong things. Or we want them for the wrong reasons. And what we want is quite often not what we need.

And it gets even more interesting. The reason we want the wrong things stems from something that happened to us earlier in life—and usually more than once. Whatever this incident was (and it doesn't have to be big), it cemented a lie about the world and our place in it. Lisa Cron calls it a misbelief. John Truby sees it as an unfulfilled need. Michael Hauge describes it as a mask we display to the world to make us feel safe—a mask that hides a deep wound from the past.

Whatever we want to call it, it is our fatal flaw, and it's directly connected to fear. From the moment that formative incident occurs, we start to see the world through these weird, distorted glasses. It's a form of self-preservation. We don't want to be wounded again. Our entire lives from then on involve (1) realizing that we're wearing these glasses, and (2) finding a way to take them off.

And just to make things even more confusing: EVERYONE wears their own pair of glasses. Everyone sees the world through their own distorted lenses that make perfect sense to them but no sense to anyone else. And they don't know it. They don't realize their entire lives are an attempt to avoid the thing they're most afraid of. They think the way they see the world and themselves is an accurate portrayal of reality. And we wonder why people don't get along.

This is life. It's the human experience. And it's at the heart of why characters either come to life on the page or flatline.

The glasses your character wears affect everything: how they see themselves and the world, the choices they make about careers and relationships, and most importantly (for your purposes), their greatest desire and their greatest fear.

They might want the right thing, but they will most certainly want it for the wrong reasons. Or they'll want the wrong thing entirely. Either way, they believe this specific and tangible thing will make them happy. Spoiler alert: they're wrong. But the whole process is gold for writers because it means their attempts to get this thing will be disastrous. Even better: they won't realize this for the bulk of the novel because they're still wearing those glasses.

Built-In Transformation

You've probably heard many times that a protagonist must change over the course of a novel. The whole idea behind wearing the wrong glasses and then taking them off builds transformation into the character arc. The character will have to change to get what they want—or to realize it's not what they need.

And when the glasses finally do come off, the protagonist will realize an important truth—either about the world or about themselves. And voilà: there's your theme.

The Internal-External Convergence

Moby-Dick by Herman Melville:
- Misbelief: Revenge will right injustices I've suffered.
- Inciting Incident: Ahab loses a boat and a leg while hunting Moby Dick.
- Goal: To get revenge on the white whale.
- Theme or Truth: Revenge is fruitless.
- Outcome: Ahab loses another boat, his life, and almost all his crew.

The Great Gatsby by F. Scott Fitzgerald:
- Misbelief: Money can buy me both love and respect.
- Inciting Incident: The woman Gatsby loves marries a rich man.
- Goal: To get rich himself in order to win her back.
- Theme or Truth: Money can't buy love or respect.
- Outcome: Gatsby gets rich, but he doesn't get love or respect.

Peter Pan by J.M. Barrie:
- Misbelief: Never growing up is my key to ultimate happiness.
- Inciting Incident: Peter Pan invites the Darling children to Neverland.
- Goal: To live forever as a child in Neverland.
- Theme or Truth: Growing up is an inevitable and essential part of life.
- Outcome: The Darling children choose to return home and grow up, while Peter stays in Neverland.

Anne of Green Gables by L.M. Montgomery:
- Misbelief: I'm unwanted because of my peculiarities.
- Inciting Incident: Anne is adopted by the Cuthberts.
- Goal: To win acceptance and find a place where she belongs.
- Theme or Truth: Individuality is a strength, not a weakness.
- Outcome: Anne is accepted and loved for who she is and finds a home in Green Gables.

A Wizard of Earthsea by Ursula K. Le Guin:
- Misbelief: Power and knowledge are the measure of who I am.
- Inciting Incident: Ged releases a shadow creature while showing off his powers.
- Goal: To defeat the shadow creature.
- Theme or Truth: True wisdom lies in understanding one's own limitations.
- Outcome: Ged accepts his shadow as part of himself, gaining wisdom and balance.

The Shining by Stephen King:
- Misbelief: I can suppress my personal demons.
- Inciting Incident: Jack Torrance becomes the winter caretaker at the Overlook Hotel.
- Goal: To provide for his family and work on his writing.
- Theme or Truth: Denial and refusal to confront personal demons can lead to self-destruction.
- Outcome: Jack is consumed by his demons (manifested by the haunted hotel), endangering his family.

Which Came First, the Character or the Plot?

Because character is what drives a plot forward, we would suggest it's more important to know your characters first before you start thinking about what they're going to do. This might be what derails most outlines in the writing process. You plan out what happens, and then you throw humanness into the mix and are surprised and dismayed when your characters come to life and take the story in directions you never intended it to go. Of course they do. They're the most important element in the story. They *are* the story. Their arc *is* the story arc.

Once you understand the essence of character arc, writing a novel becomes demystified. Critics accuse the process of being formulaic, that it simplifies human behavior too much. We would disagree. It's like saying three-act structure is formulaic. These are structural forms, yes, but the patterns have been recognized because they exist, not because they've been prescribed.

Do they work? Ask Stephen King. Look at Shakespeare. The success of these patterns has been proven countless times in great books. Three-act structure and the misbelief character arc show up in one form or another in all of them. It's not a formula so much as it is a tool for understanding the essential connection between internal and external conflict.

Is It Really That Simple? Yes and No!

Don't make the mistake of thinking this will make novel writing easy. It's never easy. But if you're working on a novel and wondering why it's failing, the chance that it's connected to character arc is approximately one hundred percent—because character arc is the foundation of the whole thing.

As for taking off your own glasses and dealing with your personal delusions? Sorry, we can't help you with that. We're still wearing ours.

Want to dive deeper into the craft of storytelling? This chapter is from our first book, **Immersion and Emotion: The Two Pillars of Storytelling**, available now on Amazon.

Acknowledgements

We wouldn't be anywhere without our wonderful clients at the Darling Axe: they ask the right questions, inspire us to dig deep for answers, and make us think about our own work in new ways.

Nor would we be anywhere without you, dear reader. Thank you for your ongoing support.

We learn to write by writing, but we also learn by reading. Every one of the books in *Story Skeleton: The Classics* taught us something about both writing and life. We are grateful to the masterful authors of these works for fearlessly leading the way on the literary path.

Kara, as always, you rock as a beta reader and proofreader. You see the things we miss and are not afraid to ask the tough questions.

Finally, a big thank you to MiblArt for their wonderful work on the cover.

About the Authors

Michelle Barker is an award-winning author and a senior editor with the Darling Axe. Her most recent novel *My Long List of Impossible Things* (2020, Annick Press) is a Junior Library Guild gold standard selection. *The House of One Thousand Eyes* (2018, Annick Press) won numerous awards, including the Amy Mathers Teen Book Award, and was named a Kirkus Best Book of the Year. She is also the author of *A Year of Borrowed Men*, finalist for the TD Canadian Children's Literature Award. Her  poetry, short fiction and non-fiction have been published in literary reviews around the world. Michelle lives in Vancouver, Canada, on the unceded territories of the Musqueam, Squamish, and Tsleil-Waututh nations. Find her at MichelleBarker.ca.

David Griffin Brown is an award-winning short fiction writer with over twenty-five years' experience as an editor. He founded DarlingAxe.com in 2018, which has grown into a collective of industry experts, dev editors, line editors, proofreaders, and beta readers, with specialists across all genres. He holds a BA in anthropology and an MFA in creative writing. David lives in Victoria, Canada, on the traditional territory of the Esquimalt and Songhees Nations. Find him on Bluesky and Threads under the handles @SeptimusBrown and @DarlingAxe.

David and Michelle are co-authors of the acclaimed *Immersion and Emotion: The Two Pillars of Storytelling*